Egypt and Bible History

From Earliest Times to 1000 B.C.

Charles F. Aling

WIPF & STOCK · Eugene, Oregon

Wipf and Stock Publishers
199 W 8th Ave, Suite 3
Eugene, OR 97401

Egypt in Bible History
From Earliest Times to 1000 B.C.
By Aling, Charles F.
Copyright © 1981 Baker Publishing Group All rights reserved.
Softcover ISBN-13: 978-1-5326-8035-9
Hardcover ISBN-13: 978-1-5326-8036-6
Publication date 3/31/2020
Previously published by Baker Publishing Group, 1981

This limited edition licensed by special permission of Baker Publishing Group.

Contents

Introduction

The Biblical Importance of Ancient Egypt

Ever since the great archaeological discoveries made in Egypt in the nineteenth and early twentieth centuries, culminating in the excavation of the virtually intact tomb of Tutankhamon in 1922, interest in the civilization along the Nile has grown rapidly. Books, both popular and scholarly, some of good quality and some of bad, have appeared in increasing numbers; and organized tours of Egypt have become commonplace. Along with general interest has come a new realization of the importance of ancient Egypt as one of the primary stages in mankind's historical development; historians writing since the pioneer work of James H. Breasted have generally acknowledged the many cultural debts which the modern Western world owes to Egypt.[1] But for the student of the Bible this is not enough. If Egyptian history is important for the study of modern civilization, its importance is compounded many times for the study of the Bible. Two aspects of this importance can be stated rather briefly.

First, Egypt was a part of the Old Testament world, just as much as were Assyria, Damascus, Babylon, and even Israel

---

1. See James H. Breasted, *A History of Egypt*, 2nd ed. (New York: Charles Scribner's Sons, 1946).

itself. The great pharaohs of the Middle Kingdom (2000 – 1786 B.C.) were the contemporaries of the patriarchs; the imperial pharaohs of the New Kingdom (1570 – 1085 B.C.), Egypt's great period of conquest and expansion, were contemporary with Moses and Joshua. Thus, if we are to understand the Word of God in its proper historical context (which is imperative), we must know something of Egyptian history and civilization. As we explore Egyptian customs and practices, portions of Israel's history such as the story of Joseph and the subsequent period of bondage become much more real to us; and, as will be seen later, unclear and seemingly insignificant verses or parts of verses appear in a new light as important references to local custom. We will note that the chronology of Scripture with respect to the career of Joseph, the length of the sojourn, and the time of the exodus fits perfectly with what is known of Egyptian history. Also we will appreciate God's sovereignty over human history, as we see Egypt's military might decline suddenly at exactly the time of the conquest of Canaan by Joshua. Finally, we will learn to refrain from misinterpretation of Scripture by avoiding the allegorical method which is sadly so common today, and which substitutes man's ideas for the clear meaning of God's Word. We will see the strength of adhering to the grammatical-historical method of interpretation. Our rewards will be many as we examine Egyptian history as an integral part of the Old Testament narrative.

Although basically outside the scope of this book, a second reason why the Bible scholar of today should be interested in Egypt is the great emphasis which the Lord gave to Egypt in the prophetic sections of His Word. Large portions of the books of Isaiah, Jeremiah, and Ezekiel deal with Egypt's prophetic future, yet few students of the Bible know or appear to care about the topic. To God it was an important subject. Note, for example, that Ezekiel has four chapters (29 – 32) dealing specifically with Egypt. It therefore behooves us as students of God's Word to know something about the nation of Egypt in Old Testament times. So let us begin!

The Geography of Egypt

Any treatment of Egypt's civilization must begin with a description of that nation's unique geographical features, since those features did so much to shape the culture of that part of the world. Egypt is located on the continent of Africa, but this is somewhat deceptive. The Sahara Desert and the impassable cataracts of the Upper Nile successfully isolated the Egyptians from the rest of Africa, and what foreign contacts occurred were with western Asia instead of Africa. Thus, the Egyptians must first be considered part of the Near East rather than part of Africa.

Once we place Egypt in the Near Eastern cultural sphere, we may begin to examine briefly three key geographical features which have influenced Egyptian civilization from time immemorial. The first of these is the Nile. This great river, flowing north from equatorial Africa to the Mediterranean, was in ancient times and is today the single most important geographical feature in Egypt, being both the source of life for all crops (rainfall is negligible in Egypt) and the major highway for all travel and transportation in Egypt. Once a year in ancient times the Nile flooded, bringing both water and rich, fertile soil deposits from far upriver. This predictable flooding and revitalizing of the soil made the Nile Valley one of the earth's richest agricultural areas. And, indeed, farming and life in general in Egypt are restricted for the most part to the Nile River Valley, which is narrow in Upper Egypt (the south) but fans out gradually in Lower Egypt (the north, commonly called the delta). The rest of Egypt as seen on the maps of today is desert. Man lives, then, on about 3 percent of what our maps call Egypt—the other 97 percent is trackless waste!

A second major geographical feature that was crucial in

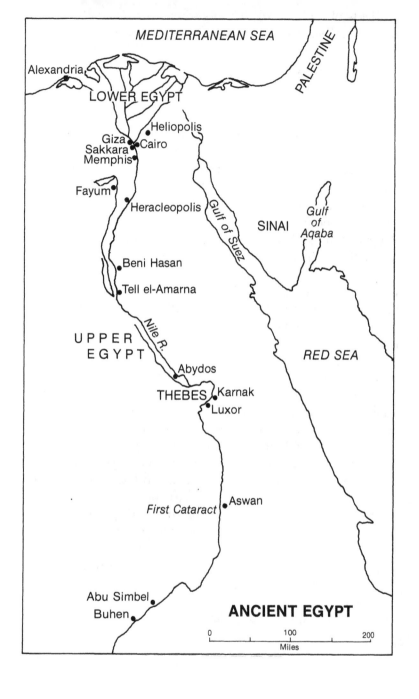

MEDITERRANEAN SEA

PALESTINE

Alexandria

LOWER EGYPT

Heliopolis

Giza
Sakkara Cairo
Memphis

Fayum

Heracleopolis

Gulf of Suez

SINAI

Gulf of Aqaba

Beni Hasan

Tell el-Amarna

UPPER EGYPT

Nile R.

RED SEA

Abydos

THEBES Karnak
Luxor

First Cataract Aswan

Abu Simbel
Buhen

ANCIENT EGYPT

0   100   200
Miles

Contrast between the desert and cultivated area.

shaping the civilization of the Nile Valley was the isolation of the area. The sea in the north, deserts in the east and west, and the cataracts of the Nile in the south, all cut foreign penetration into Egypt to a mere trickle during most periods of the nation's long history. This geographically imposed isolation allowed and encouraged the development of a unique civilization.

Finally, the geographical environment of Egypt gently but firmly molded the lifestyle. The concentration of population along the easily traveled Nile led to cultural unity. The nature of the land encouraged farming, which became (and still is today) Egypt's main means of livelihood. The lack of good timber for construction forced the Egyptians to turn to what was available and abundant—brick made from mud and eventually stone, in the use of which the Egyptians became master craftsmen.

In this land of relative safety, potential prosperity, and abundant (if limited in type) material resources, one of the great riverine civilizations developed through many centuries. By the time Abraham visited Egypt, its history was already long. Before we trace that history, we must say a few words about the study of ancient Egypt by scholars of today.

Egyptian History

Modern Egyptologists divide the history of Egypt into a series of major periods.[2] The periods of Egypt's strength are called Kingdoms; those of weakness, Intermediate Periods. Even before the first of the Kingdoms there were two periods that can be considered developmental: the Predynastic Age (4000 – 3100 B.C.) and the Archaic Period (3100 – 2800 B.C.). We then come to the first great period of Egypt, the Old Kingdom (2800 – 2200 B.C.), followed by a time of weakness called the First Intermediate Period (2200 – 2000 B.C.). The Middle Kingdom (2000 – 1786 B.C.), another great period, albeit not quite as glorious in some respects as the Old Kingdom, followed the First Intermediate Period, and was succeeded in turn by another time of difficulty called the Second Intermediate Period (1786 – 1570 B.C.). This last age is often described as the Hyksos Period, named after foreigners from Syria-Palestine who entered the delta and gradually took it over until their expulsion about 1570 B.C. Finally, we come to the greatest of all periods of Egyptian history, the New Kingdom or Empire (1570 – 1085 B.C.). During this era the Egyptians became imperialistic conquerors for the first time in their long history, annexing Syria-Palestine into an Egyptian empire.

We can further subdivide the periods of Egyptian history into numbered dynasties or groups of kings (a dynasty may or may not have been a succession of rulers from the same family line):

2. Many good histories of ancient Egypt are available in English. An excellent and nontechnical work is that of George Steindorff and Keith C. Seele, *When Egypt Ruled the East* (Chicago: University of Chicago, 1965). A more technical book is Alan H. Gardiner, *Egypt of the Pharaohs: An Introduction* (New York: Oxford University, 1966). More readable, although outdated by many recent archaeological discoveries and much research, but still a classic, is Breasted's *History.* For an analysis of Egypt's cultural development, see John A. Wilson, *The Culture of Ancient Egypt* (Chicago: University of Chicago, 1956).

Archaic Period—dynasties 1–2
Old Kingdom—dynasties 3–6
First Intermediate Period—dynasties 7–10
Middle Kingdom—dynasties 11–12
Second Intermediate Period—dynasties 13–17
New Kingdom—dynasties 18–20
Post–New Kingdom—dynasties 21 and following

A word about our sources of information is necessary at this point. How do we know anything at all about Egypt's past since the Egyptians themselves have left us not one single written "history book"? It is true that the Bible gives us some information about Egypt, but, since God never intended His Word to serve as a detailed history of a pagan people, whole periods (such as the Old Kingdom) are left out, and few kings are even named. The Bible does not speak enough about matters of Egyptian secular history for us to compile a continuous narrative. We are forced to look outside the Bible's pages for the specifics of Egyptian history.

Many classical Greek and Roman authors wrote about Egypt, some briefly and others extensively. Unfortunately, the Greeks and Romans knew very little about Egypt since that nation had already passed its time of greatness by hundreds of years when the classical writers lived. Thus, the pages of authors such as Herodotus and Diodorus Siculus provide us with garbled and distorted truth at best, and with mere folk tales current in their day at worst. The one exception is the Egyptian priest Manetho, who lived under the Ptolemies (Greek kings of Egypt after the conquest of the known world by Alexander the Great) in the third century B.C. This priest wrote a history of his native land in Greek, and seems to have known enough of the ancient hieroglyphic script to be able to utilize temple records in his research. Unhappily, Manetho's original work has not been preserved down to the present. We have only parts of it in the form of fragments quoted by later writers who were mainly interested in Manetho's lists of kings and the number of years each of those kings reigned. A further difficulty lies in the fact that the later writers who have quoted Manetho are rarely very careful about how they do so; different authors disagree in their quotation of the same passage. The usefulness of Manetho's figures for the study of Egyptian history is thus very limited; it is safest to rely on his numbers only when they are in agreement with numbers on contemporary monuments of the king in question.[3]

The decipherment of the hieroglyphic script in the early nineteenth century gave us the key which unlocks the secrets of Egypt's past. Today, scholars can read literally thousands of Egyptian records written on stone (and other materials) by the ancient Egyptians themselves. It is true, however, that these records give us a slanted picture of ancient Egypt in several ways. For one thing, because the writings were in the main intended for public consumption or to impress the gods, the records of Egypt are something less than totally candid. Never, for example, would a king or an official describe himself as anything but the greatest person ever to hold his particular office. Another distortion stems from the religious character of most of Egypt's surviving monuments. Most of what remains (although not all) is either cult buildings such as temples, or funerary structures, including tombs and related buildings. From this has come the false idea that the Egyptians were preoccupied with death and the afterlife. And yet, despite these distortions and other shortcomings (such as the almost total absence of business and legal documents) we have, thanks to the many inscriptions preserved in the dry climate of the Nile Valley, a considerable knowledge of ancient Egypt's history and culture during Old Testament times.

A Word About Chronology

Finally, a note is necessary as to how we know the dates for the kings and periods of Egyptian history. It is a fact that

3. Most modern writers who seek to revise Egyptian chronology to fit their conceptions of biblical chronology rely too heavily on Manetho's figures, without understanding the problems involved. It is wisest to base chronology on Egyptian hieroglyphic monuments, and not on the confused remains of Manetho.

we know more about the chronology of Egypt than about that of most Near Eastern nations. This is due to the Egyptians' interest in astronomy. Egyptian astronomers showed particular interest in the rising of the Dog Star Sirius (or Sothis). They were especially pleased when Sirius rose at the same time the sun rose, and even more so when this simultaneous event occurred on New Year's Day in the spring of the year. Now it is a fact known to modern astronomers that Sirius rises with the sun on the same day for four years; then its rise with the sun shifts one day later in the year, and so on through the calendar. After 1,460 years, Sirius's rise with the sun has moved through the entire year back to the day on which it started the cycle. Calculations show us that in ancient times such a cycle would have begun on the Egyptian New Year's Day in three specific sets of four years: around 4240 B.C., 2780 B.C., and 1320 B.C.

To show how all this helps us, we need but to take one specific example.[4] In a document dated to year 120 of Egypt's Twelfth Dynasty, Sirius is said to have risen with the sun on the 225th day of the year. Remembering that the rise of Sirius shifts one day later every four years, we must date this document 900 years (4 × 225) after 4240, 2780, or 1320 B.C. Of these three starting dates, only 2780 is reasonable; 2780 minus 900 yields 1880 for year 120 of Dynasty Twelve, the year of our document. And, if 1880 is year 120, the dynasty must have begun about 2000 B.C.

As a check on this astronomical method of establishing Egyptian dates, we can employ what Egyptologists call "dead reckoning": adding together the regnal years of kings from a known point in time to an unknown date. Starting from 525 B.C., the known date of the Persian conquest of Egypt, and counting back to the start of the New Kingdom, we arrive at 1577 B.C. Using the astronomical method outlined above (with the details omitted), we arrive at 1572 B.C. for the beginning of the New Kingdom, which is close enough to 1577 to show

4. Taken from James H. Breasted, *Ancient Records of Egypt* (Chicago: University of Chicago, 1906), vol. 1, par. 38ff.

us that we are substantially correct. We can indeed have confidence in the dates for Egyptian kings given us by modern scholarship. As we will see, these dates do not in any way disagree with or contradict Scripture.

1

Egyptian History Through the Time of Abraham

Events in Egypt Before Abraham

When Abraham came down to Egypt in about 2090 B.C.,[1] that country had already passed through over one thousand years of recorded history, and through another millennium of prehistoric development before that. We need not linger here on the various stages of Egypt's prehistoric (the term merely means "before writing") culture; these have been amply treated elsewhere[2] and have little biblical relevance. Suffice it to say that during Egypt's prehistory, extending roughly from 4000 to 3100 B.C., the Egyptians worshiped the same gods, lived the same kind of life, spoke (and were beginning to write) the same language, and had the seeds of the same political and social institutions that we see throughout the long history of the Nile Valley's civilization.[3] And toward the end of this formative period came one of the most significant events of all, the unification of Egypt into one kingdom (called Upper and Lower Egypt) by a shadowy Upper Egyptian king called Menes. This Menes was either the first or some other

1. On the dates for Abraham, see p. 21.
2. A good general summary of predynastic Egypt may be found in Jean Bottero, et al., *The Near East: The Early Civilizations* (New York: Delacorte, 1967), pp. 232 – 57.
3. Ibid., p. 232.

15

early ruler of what we now call Dynasty One; with him and his successors begins the recorded history of dynastic Egypt.

The Archaic Period (Dynasties One and Two, 3100 – 2800 B.C.) also has little direct biblical relevance, but saw further elaboration of those ideas and institutions formulated in pre-historic times.[4] The Archaic Period was succeeded about 2800 B.C. by the first of Egypt's truly great ages, the Old Kingdom. We must pause here to describe the grandeur of this important period.

Of the kings, events, battles, and personalities of Dynasties Three through Six we know very little.[5] The most important king of Dynasty Three was Djoser, because it was during his reign that building with large stones was initiated.[6] Djoser's vizier and chief architect Imhotep, a sort of superhuman jack-of-all-trades who was deified in later Egyptian history mainly because of his medical knowledge, is credited with inventing techniques of stone construction.[7] Imhotep built the first of the Egyptian pyramids, the step pyramid of Sakkara, as a tomb for his king. Later, the Egyptians perfected their use of stone and were able to build smooth rather than terraced pyramids.

Pyramid building reached its climax under kings Khufu (Greek, Cheops) and Khafre (Greek, Chephren) of Dynasty Four.[8] While virtually nothing is known of the reigns of Khufu or Khafre (or about most of the other kings of their dynasty) aside from the pyramids they built at Giza near modern Cairo, these structures are witness enough to the wealth and power of the Old Kingdom. The Great Pyramid, as Khufu's

4. On the period in general, see W. B. Emery, *Archaic Egypt* (Baltimore: Penguin Books, 1961). For an exciting discussion of how Egyptian civilization came of age during Dynasties One and Two, see John A. Wilson, *The Culture of Ancient Egypt* (Chicago: University of Chicago, 1956), pp. 43 – 68.

5. See Alan H. Gardiner, *Egypt of the Pharaohs: An Introduction* (New York: Oxford University, 1966), chapter 5.

6. Bottero, *Near East*, pp. 282ff.

7. On Imhotep see J. B. Hurry, *Imhotep, the Vizier and Physician of King Zoser* (Oxford: Oxford University, 1926).

8. The best discussion of Egyptian pyramids is I. E. S. Edwards, *The Pyramids of Egypt* (Baltimore: Penguin Books, 1947). For a more popular treatment see Ahmed Fakhry, *The Pyramids* (Chicago: University of Chicago, 1961).

A Fourth-Dynasty pharaoh and his queen— Menkaure and Khamerer-Nebty II. *Courtesy, Museum of Fine Arts, Boston.*

tomb has been named, was rightly classified as one of the seven wonders of the world, and contains enough blocks of stone (much of which was quarried in the immediate area) to build a wall ten feet high around France![9] Pyramids continued as the basic type of royal tomb through the rest of the Old Kingdom, but with the end of Dynasty Four their great age came to a close. The pyramids of Dynasty Five and Six were small in comparison with their Fourth-Dynasty counterparts, and have not attracted much popular attention.

The major event of Dynasty Five was religious: a new major

9. Edwards, *Pyramids*, p. 117.

The pyramids of Giza.

The Great Pyramid of Khufu.

god, the sun god Re of Heliopolis, was elevated to prominence. This event is called by historians the "Re Revolution."[10]
Before Dynasty Five the falcon god Horus had been pre-

10. Wilson, *Ancient Egypt*, pp. 87ff.

eminent, but the sun god now superseded him. Re, later to be combined with the god Amon of Thebes, remained Egypt's supreme deity until Christianity conquered the Nile Valley.

At the end of Dynasty Six (about 2200 B.C.) the central authority began to decline, and the local princes throughout the Nile Valley started to show clear signs of independence from royal control.[11] Weakened by the dual problems of decentralization and economic collapse hastened by too much government expenditure for tomb building, the Old Kingdom passed away and the First Intermediate Period began.

Culture in the Old Kingdom

The essence of political theory in the Old Kingdom was that the king was a god on earth; he was not the head of state, he was the state. Before Dynasty Five he was the embodiment of Horus, and after the Re Revolution he was also considered to be the physical son of Re. The king's word was law, and he was assisted in ruling the land by an army of officials who administered Egypt's population and agricultural wealth.

A key point to remember about the Old Kingdom is that Egypt was not in any way imperialistic as yet. The days when Egyptian armies would march south to incorporate Nubia (the modern Sudan, biblical Ethiopia) or would drive deep into Syria-Palestine lay far in the future.[12] Nor should we think of the typical Egyptian of this age as a sober, mysterious person preoccupied with death. In reality, the philosophy of the day was one of carefree, happy optimism.[13] This is revealed to us through the literature and art of the period, which depict the Egyptians as a people who enjoyed life to the full. Even the building of elaborate tombs was done to ensure a happy life in the next world, and shows just how much the Egyptians loved life. They expended every effort to prolong it even beyond the grave.

11. Bottero, *Near East*, p. 327.
12. Wilson, *Ancient Egypt*, p. 82.
13. Ibid., p. 78.

While on the subject of burial and tombs, we must pause to discuss another aspect of the study of pyramids. Some modern writers, following the lead of Charles Piazzi Smyth in the last century, have denied that the Great Pyramid of Khufu was ever intended as a tomb, but was instead a mystical structure in whose very angles of construction are hidden the secrets of the universe. Such claims are of course absurd, having not one shred of hard evidence behind them. All such theories must be viewed as the products of active modern imaginations—they have no support from Egyptian texts or from archaeology. The idea that the Great Pyramid contains hidden messages from the past for us has sadly been taken a step further by those who wish to see in this famous structure the "Bible in stone"; they attempt to trace events prophesied in Scripture in the passageways and rooms of the pyramid, and thus enter the realm of theological error. The pyramid is merely a large tomb; it is not to be equated in any way with the Bible, for there is only one source of special revelation to man—the Word of God![14]

The First Intermediate Period

Following the collapse of the strong kings of the Old Kingdom, Egypt entered upon its first time of weakness and confusion, the First Intermediate Period (2200 – 2000 B.C., Dynasties Seven through Ten). Although royal monuments from this period are relatively scarce, literary texts describing the evils of the age do exist. Some of the most important of these texts are "The Admonitions of Ipu-wer," "The Dispute of a Man with His Soul," and "The Tale of the Eloquent Peasant."[15] The same basic theme weaves its way through these literary works—the breakdown of central authority and of

14. For more detailed discussion of the pseudoscience of pyramidology see Wilbur M. Smith, *Egypt in Biblical Prophecy* (Grand Rapids: Baker, 1957), chapter 13.

15. Excellent translations of these literary works are available. See, for example, Miriam Lichtheim, *Ancient Egyptian Literature*, 2 vols. (Berkeley: University of California, 1973, 1976).

the very social fabric of Egypt.[16] To be sure, Egypt still had kings; Dynasties Seven and Eight ruled weakly from Memphis, and were followed by Dynasties Nine and Ten in Heracleopolis. But no pharaoh of this period could claim authority or prestige anything like that of the kings of the Old Kingdom.

Egyptologist Jean Vercoutter has divided this troubled age into three parts.[17] First, there is the time of the demise of the Old Kingdom, attended by Asiatic infiltration into the delta and great social upheaval. Second, following a brief period of calm under Dynasty Nine, Egypt entered a time of preparation for civil war between Dynasty Ten of Heracleopolis and the nobles who later became Dynasty Eleven of Thebes. Third, Thebes gradually conquered all rival power centers and started what historians call the Middle Kingdom.

Abraham in Egypt

The first major contact between the Hebrews and Egypt was Abraham's descent into the Nile Valley, recounted in Genesis 12:10−20. Chronologically, this visit must have occurred during the First Intermediate Period. This can be demonstrated scripturally by counting back from a known reference point, the fourth year of Solomon's reign, 966 B.C. According to I Kings 6:1, the exodus took place 480 years before Solomon's fourth year, or 1446 B.C. Jacob entered Egypt 430 years before the exodus (Exod. 12:40), or in 1876 B.C., when he was 130 years old (Gen. 47:9). Jacob's birth date was therefore 1876 plus 130, or 2006 B.C. Since Isaac was sixty when Jacob was born in 2006 (Gen. 25:26), Isaac was born in 2066 B.C.; Abraham was 100 at that time (Gen. 21:5), thus being born himself in 2166 B.C. Abraham began his migration from Ur at seventy-five (Gen. 12:4), or in 2091 B.C. His journey to Egypt presumably followed his arrival in Canaan very closely, thus fitting into Vercoutter's second stage of the First Intermediate Period.

---

16. See, for example, "The Dispute of a Man with His Soul," in Lichtheim, *Ancient Egyptian Literature*, vol. 1, pp. 163ff., in which a man debates with his soul concerning the merits of death.

17. Bottero, *Near East*, pp. 327ff.

The story of Abraham's sojourn in Egypt is well known. He descended into Egypt from Canaan because of famine, passing off his beautiful wife Sarah as his sister so that the Egyptians would not kill him and take her for themselves. The pharaoh, who in accord with normal practice in the Pentateuch is not named, seized Sarah anyway, on the recommendation of his officials, but paid Abraham for her with gifts of animals and servants. But since Sarah was Abraham's wife, God plagued the pharaoh until he gave her back to Abraham, and expelled the pair from the country. Our task is to examine these events in light of what is known about the First Intermediate Period.

In the first place, it is a generally accepted fact that during Egypt's two Intermediate Periods Asiatics entered the Nile delta relatively at will.[18] Thus, it would not be difficult for a Bedouin chieftain like Abraham to enter Egypt across borders which were not guarded as they were during times of strong central government. Motives for Asiatic infiltration are not hard to imagine; shortage of food, as was the case with Abraham, and the general attraction of Egypt's civilization are plausible explanations. Trade also was a strong reason to visit Egypt. A famous painting in the tomb of Knumhotep at Beni Hasan is often rightly cited as illustrative of Abraham's visit to Egypt, although the scene dates from the later Middle Kingdom.[19] In this colorful scene an Asiatic chief, Absha, comes to Egypt, accompanied by thirty-seven of his countrymen, bringing eye paint to trade. Such visits were evidently not uncommon during times of Egyptian strength, and can be considered even more common in times of weak border security.

If Abraham came to Egypt reasonably soon after 2091 B.C., he may have been there during the reign of Wahkare-Kheti III

18. For the First Intermediate Period see Gardiner, *Egypt of the Pharaohs*, pp. 109ff., and for the Second, John Van Seters, *The Hyksos: A New Investigation* (New Haven, CT: Yale University, 1966), chapter 7.

19. Percy E. Newberry, *Beni Hasan* (London: Kegan Paul, Trench, Trübner and Co., 1893), vol. 1, plate XXXI.

(ca. 2120 – 2070 B.C.),[20] one of the last stable rulers of Dynasty Ten. Coming, as Abraham did, from the north, he would logically have contacted a Heracleopolitan monarch rather than a prince of Thebes farther south.

We are fortunate to have a fairly long literary text, "The Instruction for King Merikare," from the days of Kheti's son and successor Merikare, the last strong king of the dynasty; the document purports to be the advice of King Kheti to the future king.[21] Although we do not know whether Kheti actually had a part in the composition of this work, and although it would be rash to state dogmatically that Kheti III was the pharaoh met by Abraham, since our chronological knowledge of the First Intermediate Period is not totally firm, the material contained in the "Instruction" certainly sheds light on times not far removed from, and very possibly contemporary with, Abraham's descent into Egypt. Thus we may glean some hints about what Egypt was like in Abraham's day, and about what was considered proper kingly behavior in that time. Kings are exhorted to be just, first in their punishment of criminals, and also, more to the point in the case of Abraham, in respecting the property of others. King Merikare is challenged: "Do justice, then you endure on earth; calm the weeper, don't oppress the widow, don't expel a man from his father's property, don't reduce the nobles in their possessions."[22] While these injunctions obviously refer to native Egyptian nobles, it is clear that unrightful seizure of another's property by the king was considered wrong. We see the pharaoh's guilt reflected in his attempt to pay Abraham for his "sister" (Gen. 12:16), and finally in Sarah's release when the king finds out he has seized another man's wife.

Another text of the First Intermediate Period, "The Tale of the Eloquent Peasant,"[23] amplifies the theme of the unrightful seizure of property even further than does the "Instruction." A farmer from the Wadi Natrum area just outside Egypt

---

20. The dates are Vercoutter's, in Bottero, *Near East*, p. 334.
21. Lichtheim, *Ancient Egyptian Literature*, vol. 1, pp. 97ff.
22. Ibid., p. 100.
23. Ibid., pp. 170ff.

goes down to the Nile Valley for food, just as Abraham did. He takes trade goods with him, loaded on the backs of his donkeys; but in Egypt he is met by a rapacious official who seizes his donkeys on a false pretext. The peasant addresses nine eloquent appeals to the king's chief steward in an effort to have his property returned, and he is finally successful. Two things become obvious to us from this story. Unlawful seizure of property by government officials was a real possibility, or the account would not have been believable to its Egyptian audience. Also, arbitrary confiscation of private property was considered wrong, as the ending of the story clearly testifies (the guilty official is seized by the chief steward, and his property in turn is handed over to the wronged peasant).

The story of Abraham's temporary loss of Sarah in Egypt is, then, perfectly understandable in the turbulent setting of the First Intermediate Period.[24] Abraham did not remain in the land of the pharaohs but returned to Canaan; it would be more than two centuries before another Hebrew, Joseph, under very different circumstances, was to enter Egypt.

24. On Abraham's reception of camels from the pharaoh, long considered anachronistic, see the evidence presented in Harold G. Stigers, *A Commentary on Genesis* (Grand Rapids: Zondervan, 1975), p. 143.

2

Joseph's Early Years

The Middle Kingdom

The conquest of all Egypt by the Theban Eleventh Dynasty inaugurated a second great age of Egyptian civilization, the Middle Kingdom (2000 – 1786 B.C.). Under Dynasty Eleven power was consolidated in the hands of one family of kings from Thebes, some of whom took the name Mentuhotep.[1] The third and last of the Mentuhoteps was succeeded by his vizier Amenemhat, who became the founder of Dynasty Twelve, the most important group of rulers of the Middle Kingdom. Eight pharaohs (including one woman—Sebeknefru) comprise the dynasty:[2]

Amenemhat I	1991 – 1962
Sesostris I	1971 – 1928
Amenemhat II	1929 – 1895
Sesostris II	1897 – 1878
Sesostris III	1878 – 1843
Amenemhat III	1842 – 1797
Amenemhat IV	1798 – 1790
Sebeknefru	1789 – 1786

1. Jean Bottero et al., *The Near East: The Early Civilizations* (New York: Delacorte, 1967), pp. 347ff.
2. The dates are those of William C. Hayes, *The Middle Kingdom of Egypt* (New York: Cambridge University, 1964). Our brief account of the Twelfth Dynasty is based on pp. 34ff.

After consolidating his power, the aged Amenemhat I associated his son Sesostris with him as coregent, a common practice in Dynasty Twelve. Together these co-kings began one of the major projects of the Middle Kingdom, the conquest of Nubia, a task that was to occupy the attention of many of their successors.

The reign of Amenemhat I ended with his assassination; but Sesostris I continued the vigorous policies of his father, especially in regard to the incorporation of northern Nubia into the kingdom. His armies pushed their way as far south as Buhen at the second cataract of the Nile. At home, Sesostris I was a prolific builder. Monuments at no fewer than thirty-five sites throughout the Nile Valley stand as eloquent witnesses to his power and energy.

Under Amenemhat II and Sesostris II further wars in the south were unnecessary; trade seems to have been Egypt's major concern. There is evidence of extensive foreign trade during this time between Egypt and most parts of the ancient world; the result must have been great prosperity.

By all accounts Sesostris III was the most important ruler of the Twelfth Dynasty. The conquest and pacification of Nubia, neglected for two generations, were begun again on a grand scale. In a series of campaigns (some led by Sesostris himself) the southern border of Egypt was extended to Semna, and a string of fortresses was built to solidify Egyptian strength in the south.

Also of interest are certain administrative reforms made by Sesostris III. Amenemhat I, in establishing a new dynasty, had been forced to depend upon the powerful nobles of the nomes (districts) of Egypt for support. Under Amenemhat and his successors these nobles were granted increased power and even a measure of independence in return for their support of the dynasty. But Sesostris III would not tolerate the resultant growth of the nomarchs' power and the corresponding decline of his own authority. Although details are not known, it is clear that Sesostris III broke the power of these officials and transferred their authority to many newly created positions.

Amenemhat III did not need to be a great warrior; his father had done all the fighting necessary to bring peace to the land. Under Amenemhat Egypt reached the highest level of prosperity attained during the Middle Kingdom. His reign was one of rapid economic expansion, including massive exploitation of mines and quarries, foreign trade, and, most interesting, a large-scale land reclamation project in the Fayum region to the west of the Nile.

The last two pharaohs of the dynasty were Amenemhat IV and his sister Sebeknefru.[3] Amenemhat IV appears to have been a strong ruler, but Sebeknefru was not. Little is known of her brief reign; after her death power slipped into the hands of a family of former viziers who became Dynasty Thirteen. The great days of the Middle Kingdom were over.

In literature and the arts, the Middle Kingdom was a classic age. Many of the greatest literary masterpieces of all Egyptian history come from Dynasty Twelve.[4] Among the most famous are the "Story of the Shipwrecked Sailor," a fanciful tale about the adventures of a sailor marooned on an island inhabited by a giant serpent, and the "Story of Sinuhe," the semifactual account of an official who fled Egypt at the time of the assassination of Amenemhat I.[5] These and other literary works of the same period are written in Middle Egyptian, the classical form of the long-lived Egyptian language.

In art and architecture also the surviving examples from the Middle Kingdom show us that this was a truly great time for Egypt.[6] Relief sculpture, statuary, forts, temples, and paintings are all witnesses to the skill of Middle Kingdom craftsmen. The kings built brick pyramids, but these are poor examples of funerary architecture; most of them are shapeless piles of rubble today.

3. William C. Hayes, *Egypt: From the Death of Ammenemes III to Seqnenre II* (New York: Cambridge University, 1962), pp. 3 – 4.

4. See Hayes, *Middle Kingdom*, pp. 62 – 70, for an excellent summary of Middle Kingdom literature.

5. Miriam Lichtheim, *Ancient Egyptian Literature*, 2 vols. (Berkeley: University of California, 1973, 1976), vol. 1, pp. 211, 222.

6. For a brief survey see Hayes, *Middle Kingdom*, pp. 51ff.

Middle Kingdom shrine at Karnak.

In religion, the Middle Kingdom saw the rise to prominence of several new gods,[7] the most important of which was
Amon of Thebes, who was equated with Re and made into
a new composite deity called Amon-Re. Also newly important
in the Middle Kingdom were Montu, a falcon-headed war
god of Thebes, and Sebek, the crocodile deity of the Fayum
region. Another religious development of this age was what
William C. Hayes calls the "democratization of the hereafter,"
the belief that Egyptians other than the king and his highest
officials could have a part in the afterlife.[8] The catch was, of
course, a financial one. The lowliest subject of the pharaoh
might gain immortality, but only if he could afford to buy the
appropriate magical spells.

Joseph's Entrance into Egypt

Before we investigate the years spent by Joseph in Egypt,
a word of caution is necessary. We should not expect to find

---

7. Ibid., pp. 57ff.
8. Ibid., pp. 59ff.

Egyptian references to Joseph or even necessarily to specific events in the biblical record, for secular sources of information are relatively few, and our knowledge of private individuals in this period is scanty.

We may rather expect results of two other kinds. First, we can expect to obtain a wealth of illustrative background information which shows us what Egypt was like in Joseph's day. Such information brings the Bible into better focus; we see it as a book of real people living in a real and colorful world. Second, and perhaps more important, we may expect to illuminate and explain obscure portions of the biblical narrative, portions we cannot fully understand outside of an Egyptian context.

As we have already seen (p. 21), according to the biblical chronology Jacob's migration into Egypt must be dated to approximately 1876 B.C. Since Joseph had already been there for some time, a Middle Kingdom date for his sale into Egyptian slavery is required.[9] This fact is in contradiction to most current scholarly opinion, which places the career of Joseph in the Second Intermediate Period, under the Asiatic Hyksos who ruled in the delta region for a number of years after the end of the Middle Kingdom.[10] This view rests on two arguments. The first is a statement of Josephus drawn from Manetho that Joseph was in Egypt under the Hyksos.[11] A second argument is that since Joseph was an Asiatic, it would be logical for him to rise to power when fellow Asiatics ruled in Egypt.[12] Neither of these arguments is strong and neither fits the biblical chronology. It is best to disregard Josephus unless

9. See James R. Battenfield, "A Consideration of the Identity of the Pharaoh of Genesis 47," *Journal of the Evangelical Theological Society* 15 (Spring, 1972): 77 – 85.

10. Among Egyptologists see W. M. F. Petrie, *Egypt and Israel* (London: Society for Promoting Christian Knowledge, 1911), p. 27; T. Eric Peet, *Egypt and the Old Testament* (Liverpool: University of Liverpool, 1924), chapter 4; and, more recently, Kenneth A. Kitchen, "Joseph," in *New Bible Dictionary,* ed. J. D. Douglas (Grand Rapids: Eerdmans, 1962), p. 657. Among biblical scholars, see the full discussion with bibliography in John Bright, *A History of Israel,* 2nd ed. (Philadelphia: Westminster, 1972), chapters 2 and 3.

11. Josephus *Against Apion* 1. 14.

12. Peet, *Egypt,* p. 73.

there is archaeological confirmation of his assertions, and it is best not to link Joseph to the Hyksos just because both came from Syria-Palestine. As we will see, the details given in Genesis fit far better with the Middle Kingdom than with the Second Intermediate Period.

As to Joseph's exact date within the Middle Kingdom, James R. Battenfield has collated the biblical information with the accepted chronology of the Middle Kingdom.[13] In summary, Joseph was sold into slavery in approximately 1897 B.C., during the last years of Amenemhat II. It was then Sesostris II who first imprisoned and later elevated Joseph to a position of power in about 1884 B.C.; but since that pharaoh died in 1878, the bulk of Joseph's career belongs in the reign of the great king Sesostris III.

In recent years a great deal of study has been given to the subject of slavery, and of Asiatic slaves particularly, in ancient Egypt.[14] The number of Syro-Palestinian slaves in Egypt grew steadily during the late years of Dynasty Twelve and during all of Dynasty Thirteen. While some of the Asiatic slaves were without doubt prisoners seized by the Egyptians during raids into Palestine,[15] many must have entered Egypt by means of a slave trade. This is indicated, according to both German Egyptologist Wolfgang Helck and Hayes, by the predominance of female slaves over male in our extant source material.[16] If most of the foreign slaves began their servitude as prisoners of war, we would expect to find an excess of male rather than female slaves. While it is true that there are no

13. Battenfield, "Identity of the Pharaoh," pp. 84 – 85.

14. On Egyptian slavery in general see A. Bakir, *Slavery in Pharaonic Egypt* (Cairo: L'Institut Français d'archéologie orientale, 1952). On Asiatics see John Van Seters, *The Hyksos: A New Investigation* (New Haven, CT: Yale University, 1966), pp. 90ff.; William C. Hayes, ed., *A Papyrus of the Late Middle Kingdom in the Brooklyn Museum*, Wilbour Monographs 5 (Brooklyn: Brooklyn Museum, 1972 reprint); and G. Posener, "Les Asiatiques en Egypte sous les XIIe et XIIIe Dynasties," *Syria* 34 (1957): 145 – 63.

15. Van Seters, *Hyksos*, pp. 90 – 91.

16. Wolfgang Helck, *Die Beziehungen Aegyptens zu Vorderasien im 3. und 2. Jahrtausend vor Christi* (Wiesbaden: Otto Harrassowitz, 1971), p. 78; and Hayes, *Papyrus*, p. 99.

preserved records of a slave trade,[17] this cannot be used as evidence that such a trade did not exist. If, as the biblical record indicates, the slave trade was in the hands of Asiatics and not Egyptians, there were probably few if any records kept by Egyptian scribes. Further, any such records would have been kept on papyrus, and the chances of examples surviving to the present day would be minimal, since the trade would have been concentrated in the delta close to the frontier, an area whose climate is not conducive to the preservation of papyri.

As an illustration of the profusion of Asiatic slaves in Middle Kingdom Egypt we need but look at the long list of slaves on one papyrus published in 1955 by Hayes.[18] Over half of the slaves listed are Asiatics; the rest are native Egyptians. The papyrus, which dates from the late Twelfth Dynasty, is evidence that Palestinian slaves like Joseph were common in Egypt at that time.

Joseph in Potiphar's House

Potiphar the Egyptian

When Joseph reached Egypt, he was purchased by an Egyptian official called Potiphar (Gen. 37:36). As the previously mentioned papyrus shows, there is nothing unusual in this purchase; private individuals (not just the king) could and did own slaves during the Middle Kingdom.[19] But before we examine Joseph's servitude in Potiphar's household, we must consider Potiphar himself. His name and titles present us with a series of difficult problems.

The first difficulty is the name Potiphar itself. Virtually all scholars are agreed that the Hebrew word *Potiphar* is the equivalent of Egyptian *pa di pa Ra*, meaning "the one whom [the god] Re has given."[20] The problem with this name cen-

17. Van Seters, *Hyksos*, p. 91.

18. Brooklyn Papyrus 35.1446—Hayes, *Papyrus*, pp. 87, 92ff.

19. Ibid., pp. 133 – 34.

20. For discussion, see J. Vergote, *Joseph en Egypte*, Orientalia et Biblica Lovaniensia III (Louvain, 1959), pp. 146 – 48.

ters around the word *pa*, the Egyptian definite article, which occurs twice in Potiphar. The use of *pa* alone in personal names is almost, but not totally, a late development, rarely occurring in the Middle Kingdom. Hermann Ranke in his authoritative study of Egyptian personal names lists 727 names with *pa* as the first element; of these only fifteen date from earlier than the New Kingdom.[21] A name beginning with *pa* is therefore unlikely, but not impossible, in the Middle Kingdom. The theory that Potiphar is a personal name passes from the realm of the unlikely to that of the impossible, however, when we consider the combination *pa* + *di* + divine name. Of 109 names which exemplify this formula (*pa* + *di* + divine name) one comes from Dynasty Eighteen and one from Dynasty Nineteen—all the rest are known only from extremely late periods of Egyptian history (after 1000 B.C.). Not one example comes from as early as Dynasty Twelve.

Several solutions to the name problem have been proposed,[22] but no scholar has been able to explain a man's having a name with a grammatical construction not otherwise attested until nearly a thousand years after he lived. The best solution is to understand "Potiphar" as a descriptive epithet meaning "one who is placed on earth by Re" (i.e., an Egyptian), and not as a name at all.

In support of this we note that it would be surprising to find a name in the Genesis account. Only two Egyptian men are "named" in the entire story of Joseph, Potiphar and Joseph's father-in-law Potiphera. No pharaoh is named in the Genesis narrative. Now it is odd that the names of these two individuals are given while no one else is accorded that privilege; and it is doubly odd when we realize that both names

21. Hermann Ranke, *Die Aegyptische Personennamen* (Glückstadt: J. J. Augustin, 1935), vol. 1, pp. 99–129.

22. The view of Kenneth A. Kitchen, "Potiphar" and "Potipherah," in *New Bible Dictionary*, ed. J. D. Douglas (Grand Rapids: Eerdmans, 1962), p. 1012, that Potiphar is a Mosaic modernization of an older type of name does not seem convincing; on the other hand, the view of Joseph P. Free, *Archaeology and Bible History* (Wheaton, IL: Scripture Press, 1962), pp. 77–78, that the names found in the story of Joseph can occur "early," is not valid for the construction *pa*+*di*+ divine name.

are variations of the same Egyptian phrase, *pa di pa Ra*.[23] These strange facts cast doubt on regarding Potiphar and Potiphera as names.

Further, the meaning of *pa di pa Ra* is significant. The idea conveyed by the phrase is that the individual was placed on earth by Re, and was in a manner of speaking the offspring of that deity. Something similar occurs elsewhere in the Old Testament. Shamgar, one of the minor judges, is called the son of Anath in Judges 3:31 and 5:6. Since the name Shamgar is probably foreign,[24] there is a strong possibility that he was not a Hebrew. The phrase "son of Anath," then, may mean that Shamgar was a member of a nationality that worshiped the Canaanite goddess Anath. The phrases "son of Anath" and "the one placed on earth by Re" would be similar in that they designate the national origin of the men so described. Potiphar thus may be merely a phrase stressing the fact that the man who bought Joseph was an Egyptian, and not a name at all, any more than the phrase "son of Anath" is a name. This explanation removes the chronological impossibility discussed above, for a *pa di* phrase so understood would be acceptable in a document written by Moses in about 1400 B.C.

A second problem regarding Potiphar is his pair of titles, officer (*sārîs*) of the pharaoh and captain of the guard (*sar haṭabbāḥîm*), given in Genesis 37:36 and 39:1. *Sārîs* is often taken to mean eunuch,[25] but this seems unlikely for two reasons: Potiphar was a married man,[26] and also, as far as we know, eunuchs were very rare in ancient Egypt.[27] The solution to this difficulty is to translate *sārîs* as officer and not eunuch at all. This fits both the Egyptian practices of the day and the use of the term *sārîs* and related words in Semitic

23. Kitchen, "Potiphar" and "Potipherah," p. 1012.

24. See F. F. Bruce, "Shamgar," in *New Bible Dictionary*, ed. J. D. Douglas (Grand Rapids: Eerdmans, 1962), p. 1170.

25. H. C. Leupold, *Exposition of Genesis* (Grand Rapids: Baker, 1965), vol. 2, p. 974. See also the detailed study of Gerald E. Kadish, "Eunuchs in Ancient Egypt?" *Studies in Honor of John A. Wilson*, Studies in Ancient Oriental Civilization 35 (Chicago: University of Chicago, 1969), pp. 55 – 62.

26. John J. Davis, *Paradise to Prison* (Grand Rapids: Baker, 1975), p. 269.

27. Kadish, "Eunuchs," p. 61.

languages (it is even possible that *sārīs* can be equated with the Egyptian word *sr* [official],[28] but such an equation is not universally accepted). In Babylonian documents the term *ša rēši*, or *sārīs*, is used to mean official, and there is no evidence that it has anything to do with eunuchs. Only in the specialized use of the Assyrians does the term mean eunuch;[29] it is not correct to carry this meaning over into Hebrew. *Sārīs* in the story of Joseph means simply officer.

The second title, *sar haṭabbāḥim*, is more difficult to interpret. Most probably it refers to some type of commander of royal bodyguards,[30] but establishing an exact Egyptian counterpart is too problematic for us to be dogmatic. In any case, it is certain that the pharaohs of the Middle Kingdom had bodyguards, since the term "bodyguard of the king" is known from as far back as the Old Kingdom,[31] and is thus not out of place in the story of Joseph. Also, the fact that the pharaoh's guard commander was a native Egyptian casts extreme doubt on the theory that the story of Joseph is to be dated in the Hyksos Period—it does not seem probable that a foreign pharaoh would have had an Egyptian, a member of a conquered race, in such a post.

The Positions Held by Joseph Under Potiphar

According to Genesis 39:2−3 Joseph began his career in Egypt as a household slave of Potiphar. Recent historical research has shed a great deal of light on this aspect of Joseph's life. From monuments of the Middle Kingdom Helck has compiled a list of Asiatic slaves which presents a striking parallel to Joseph's employment.[32] Of forty-eight Asiatics

28. Adolf Erman and Hermann Grapow, *Wörterbuch der Aegyptischen Sprache* (Berlin: Akademie Verlag, 1926 − 1931), vol. 4, p. 188.

29. John A. Brinkman, *A Political History of Post-Kassite Babylonia*, Analecta Orientalia 43 (Rome, 1968), pp. 308 − 11.

30. William A. Ward, "Egyptian Titles in Genesis 39 − 50," *Bibliotheca Sacra* 114 (January, 1957): 41. For a view that the title refers to someone involved with the royal food supply, see Vergote, *Joseph en Egypte*, pp. 31ff.

31. Erman and Grapow, *Wörterbuch*, vol. 4, p. 340.

32. Helck, *Beziehungen*, p. 77, n.2.

listed, only six have specific titles: four are called cupbearer (butler), and two are listed as domestic servants of their masters, thus holding posts identical to that of Joseph in Genesis 39:2. Helck has also tabulated the Asiatics listed in the papyrus we discussed on page 31:[33] two were domestic servants, one was a brewer, two were cooks, and one was a teacher.[34] We thus find that of those foreign slaves whose specific jobs are given in our source material, Asiatic household servants were among the most common in Egypt during the Middle Kingdom. Joseph fits the pattern well, beginning his servitude as a domestic servant alongside others of his nationality.

Like most high Egyptian officials, Potiphar evidently had agricultural estates. In Joseph he recognized the makings of an able steward for those estates, and, after a period of time, promoted him to be over all his possessions (Gen. 39:4). The Egyptian phrase for steward is "the one who is over the house," with the term *house* having the broader meaning of estate.[35]

Regarding the specific duties of a steward, we may turn to several holders of the office in the better-documented New Kingdom (1570 — 1085 B.C.) and examine their subsidiary titles. A certain Djehuty like Joseph was steward of a high governmental official, Mery, who was the high priest of Amon under Amenhotep II. A funerary cone of Djehuty[36] records that he was scribe of offerings (this shows that he was literate) and chief of agricultural slaves.[37] Another high priest of Amon had a scribe and steward named Amenhotep, again obviously

33. Hayes, *Papyrus,* p. 103.

34. Helck, *Beziehungen,* p. 78.

35. Alan H. Gardiner, *Ancient Egyptian Onomastica* (Oxford: Oxford University, 1947), vol. 1, p. 46 .

36. Norman de Garis Davies, *A Corpus of Inscribed Egyptian Funerary Cones* (Oxford: Oxford University, 1957), vol. 1, no. 402.

37. For a discussion of the term see Bakir, *Slavery,* pp. 25 — 27. Bakir concludes, despite the fact that those designated by this term were sometimes domestic servants, that they "may rightly be regarded as slaves put to work especially on land" (p. 27).

a literate man.[38] One of Egypt's viziers had a scribe, steward, and chief of agricultural slaves named Amenemhat.[39] It is quite clear from these examples that the office of steward was fairly common in the households of Egypt's great officials and that literacy was one of the prerequisites for the job. It is also clear that one of the major areas of responsibility of these men was supervision of agricultural slaves on the estates of their masters and of agricultural work in general. The remark at the end of Genesis 39:5 that everything that Potiphar had was blessed, including his possessions in the field, refers to Joseph's supervision of agriculture, and thus is a touch of authentic detail. But further, we see in Joseph's position as a supervisor of agriculture that the Lord prepared him for his remarkable achievements in the upcoming days of famine.[40]

Joseph in Prison

The next episode in Joseph's life is a familiar one; Potiphar's wife attempts to lure Joseph into an adulterous relationship, and, failing in her attempt, accuses her husband's steward of the very sin that he resisted (Gen. 39:7–20). Joseph is thrown into prison on her false charges.

The Egyptian "Tale of Two Brothers,"[41] which centers around a similar attempted seduction of an honorable man by a married woman who then accuses him of immorality, has been cited as the inspiration for the incident of Joseph and Potiphar's wife.[42] But this most certainly is not the case. Despite the similarity of motif, there are major differences between the fictional Egyptian work and the biblical ac-

38. Davies, *Corpus*, vol. 1, no. 123.

39. Ibid., no. 128.

40. Vergote's view (*Joseph en Egypte*, p. 98) that Joseph was concerned only with interior household duties can certainly not be correct.

41. Lichtheim, *Ancient Egyptian Literature*, vol. 2, pp. 203–11.

42. See *Ancient Near Eastern Texts Relating to the Old Testament*, ed. James B. Pritchard (Princeton, NJ: Princeton University, 1950), p. 23.

count.[43] Tales of this kind circulated widely in the ancient Near East; there need not be any connection at all between the story of Joseph and the "Tale of Two Brothers."[44] Beyond the realm of fiction, we find references to adultery and its punishments in Egyptian wisdom literature.[45]

In any case, Joseph was wrongfully cast into prison.[46] The papyrus with which we are already familiar provides us with abundant information about Egyptian prisons and their purposes. The prison was most commonly called the *khenret*, literally the "place of confinement."[47] It included both a fortress made up of cells like a modern prison and a sort of labor-camp barracks; prisoners were often used as forced labor. Like their modern counterparts, Egyptian prisons were filled with convicted criminals serving for a specific period of time determined by the criminal courts. But there were also individuals awaiting execution. Joseph was apparently serving a sentence of a specified number of years, while the butler and the baker were awaiting execution.

The Egyptian Great Prison at Thebes, particularly prominent in the Middle Kingdom (and perhaps, but not certainly, the actual prison of Joseph's confinement), had a full staff of officials, mainly scribes and guards, under the supervision of an overseer of the prison. Instances of the use of this title are somewhat rare, but there are examples from the time of Joseph, including the reference in Genesis 39:21 to "the keeper of the prison." Since Joseph was literate, having been a steward, it is not inconceivable that he became a scribe of the

---

43. For example, in the biblical account Joseph and Potiphar are not brothers, nor are there any mythological elements. For a complete list of differences see Harold G. Stigers, *A Commentary on Genesis* (Grand Rapids: Zondervan, 1975), p. 284.

44. This conclusion is reached by no less a critic than D. B. Redford, *A Study of the Biblical Story of Joseph* (Leiden: E. J. Brill, 1970), p. 93.

45. Vergote, *Joseph en Egypte*, pp. 22 – 24.

46. Although the normal punishment for adultery was death; see Vergote, *Joseph en Egypte*, p. 24.

47. Our information on Egyptian prisons is drawn from Hayes, *Papyrus*, pp. 37 – 42.

prison as a result of the promotion mentioned in Genesis 39:22.[48]

While in prison, Joseph met the royal butler and the royal baker, who were seemingly awaiting execution for some offense. Both titles are amply attested. The butler was literally the cupbearer of the king, a term which fits the Hebrew *mashqeh* (the one who furnishes drink) better than does our English word *butler*.[49] J. Vergote in his study of the story of Joseph cites an example of a cupbearer of the king in the Middle Kingdom.[50]

Baker was also a common title in the Middle Kingdom; but it is not possible to determine exactly what is entailed by the title in Genesis, since there were three different Egyptian words for baker in use during the Middle Kingdom.[51] In any case, the post was obviously a necessary one since bread was one of the staples of the Egyptian diet.[52]

Both men dreamt while in prison, and Joseph interpreted their dreams for them. The butler, who dreamt of grapevines and squeezing grape juice once again into the pharaoh's cup, would be returned to his post; and so he was. The baker, who saw birds eating baked goods from baskets on his head, would lose his head. His dream also came to pass. From Dynasty Nineteen (ca. 1300 B.C.) comes an Egyptian book on dream interpretation.[53] While no exact parallels to the dreams of the butler or baker are present in this work, we can learn two things from the book. The Egyptians, at least by Dynasty Nineteen but probably earlier as well, believed dreams could help foretell the future. Also, we find that the meaning of dreams was thought to be allegorical, just as in this part of the story of Joseph. Seeing a large cat, for example, meant that a plentiful harvest was coming. On the other hand, a dream about catching birds was considered an evil omen—

---

48. Ward, "Egyptian Titles," p. 43.
49. Ibid.
50. Vergote, *Joseph en Egypte*, p. 33.
51. Erman and Grapow, *Wörterbuch*, vol. 6, p. 17.
52. For an interesting discussion see Ward, "Egyptian Titles," p. 45.
53. For some excerpts, see *Ancient Near Eastern Texts*, p. 495.

it meant that the dreamer would lose his property. Or, if one dreamed of seeing one's own face in a mirror, the obtaining of another wife was predicted.

Despite his promise to tell the pharaoh of Joseph, the butler totally forgot his friend in prison when he was restored to favor. Before the next series of important events in his life, Joseph had to wait two long years in prison.

3

Joseph's Rise to Prominence

Joseph Before Pharaoh

While Joseph languished in prison, forgotten completely by the restored butler, the king of Egypt (without much doubt Sesostris II) had a recurrent dream. Before considering that dream, a word about the king's title is in order. The Egyptian term transliterated "pharaoh," meaning literally "great house," was used in Joseph's day and earlier only as a designation for the palace and never for the king personally. We must remember, however, that Moses and not Joseph is the author of the Genesis account, and Moses lived in Dynasty Eighteen (see chapter 5); it was during that dynasty that the term *pharaoh* began to be used as a personal title of the king. The earliest preserved example of the king's being addressed directly as pharaoh comes from the reign of Akhenaton (early fourteenth century B.C.), shortly after Moses' death.[1] Thus the biblical usage conforms to the practice current at the time of authorship; Egypt's king in Joseph's day is described by Moses in terms familiar to his own day. It is also interesting that Moses nowhere uses the title *pharaoh* in conjunction with a proper name, as Jeremiah does when he refers to

1. See Alan H. Gardiner, *Egyptian Grammar: Being an Introduction to the Study of Hieroglyphics*, 3rd rev. ed. (New York: Oxford University, 1957), p. 75.

kings of Egypt, for example, in the case of Pharaoh Hophra (Jer. 44:30). Such usage was common in Jeremiah's day, but would have been out of place in an earlier document.

Pharaoh's persistent dreams are familiar to all students of the Bible, and need not detain us here.[2] He dreamt of seven lean cattle devouring seven well-fed ones, and seven poor ears of grain consuming seven good ears. The magicians (ḥar-ṭōm) of Egypt were unable to interpret the king's dreams (Gen. 41:8). This Hebrew word is obviously borrowed from the Egyptian term for magician (ḥry-tp), a title designating one versed in sorcery, the black arts, and the evidently immense body of literature that had grown up around these subjects. These magicians also had connections with the House of Life, the place of compilation, study, and storage of Egypt's learned literature, a fact which helps explain the reference to wise men in the same verse.[3]

At this point in the narrative (Gen. 41:9ff.) the restored butler remembered how Joseph had correctly interpreted both his dream and that of the baker, and recommended the skills of his fellow prisoner to the king. Pharaoh sent for Joseph, but some preparation was necessary before an audience could take place. Before approaching the pharaoh, Joseph had to shave and change his clothes (Gen. 41:14). The change of clothes presumably relates to cleanliness, a matter of great importance to the ancient Egyptians. If we may believe the account of the Greek writer Herodotus (fifth century B.C.), the Egyptians abhorred lice, washed their clothes and bodies regularly, and shaved often for cleanliness' sake.[4] In regard to the shaving, we have but to look at the vast number of extant Egyptian paintings and statues in order to see that the Egyptians practiced the removal of facial hair and even the complete shaving of the head. In one well-known tomb painting

2. A detailed discussion may be found in J. Vergote, Joseph en Egypte, Orientalia et Biblica Lovaniensia III (Louvain, 1959), pp. 48ff.

3. Adolf Erman, A Handbook of Egyptian Religion (London: Archibald Constable and Co., 1907), p. 160.

4. Herodotus Histories 2. 35 – 36.

Barbers at work.

there is even a glimpse of Egyptian barbers at work and of men waiting to be served.[5]

After being made presentable, Joseph went before the pharaoh and interpreted the dreams, forecasting seven years of plenty followed by seven years of famine, and recommended that a wise man be placed in charge of preparations for the coming famine. The overseer would, in following Joseph's advice, gather up one-fifth of the land's produce during the good years for distribution in the time of shortage. Pharaoh recognized God's wisdom in this plan and appointed Joseph to be the official responsible for implementing the program. Joseph was put in charge of the pharaoh's house and made ruler over all the land of Egypt, second only to the pharaoh himself (Gen. 41:40—41). He was given the pharaoh's ring, linen robes, a gold chain to be worn around his neck (v. 42), and a chariot (v. 43).

Of the three gifts mentioned in Genesis 41:42, the gold collar occurs frequently in Egyptian artistic representations. D. B. Redford cites thirty-two examples of tomb paintings showing the king granting gold necklaces to loyal officials.[6]

5. The scene is in the tomb of Userhat at Thebes. *The Ancient Near East in Pictures*, ed. James B. Pritchard (Princeton, NJ: Princeton University, 1955), fig. 80.

6. D. B. Redford, *A Study of the Biblical Story of Joseph* (Leiden: E. J. Brill, 1970), pp. 208ff.

Egyptian official wearing a gold chain.

Redford correctly draws two conclusions about these paintings. First, none of them have anything to do with induction into high office, but on the contrary depict presentations of rewards, and second, at least in the period before the Amarna Age (fourteenth century B.C.), the rewards were given for actual service performed. Redford also concludes, however, that since gold was given as a reward for service and not as a symbol of induction into office, the biblical account does not reflect Egyptian custom. But why must we regard all of Genesis 41:37−46 as a description of Joseph's investiture? It seems better to view the formal investiture as ending with verse 41 (the pharaoh's statement that he has established Joseph as ruler over Egypt), and to take verse 42 as a description of Joseph's rewards for explaining the king's dreams.

The chariot mentioned in verse 43 might also be thought problematic, since the Egyptians did not use the horse-drawn war chariot earlier than the New Kingdom (1570 − 1085 B.C.). But need we conclude that chariots were common in Joseph's day, or even that they were then being used as weapons of war simply because Joseph received one from the pharaoh? The wording of verse 43, that Joseph was given the pharaoh's second chariot, implies that such vehicles were not common, and suggests that even the king had very few of them. Nor is anything ever said in the story of Joseph about chariots (Joseph's or anyone else's) being used in battle. There is reason to believe that the Egyptians could have had a small number of chariots during the Middle Kingdom, since there is in fact some evidence at least regarding horses. John Van Seters, in his study of the Hyksos (invaders of Egypt after the Middle Kingdom), mentions that the skeleton of a horse was found by the excavators of the Middle Kingdom fortress at Buhen.[7] Since the horse was obviously known, there may have been chariots as well, at least in limited numbers and for limited uses.

As a final gift, Joseph received an Egyptian name and an Egyptian wife, Asenath, daughter of Potiphera, priest of On. As for Joseph's name ($Spnt\ p'nh$ in Hebrew), scholars have reached no certain conclusion about the Egyptian original.[8] Perhaps the best suggestion to date is that of Leibovitch, who has posited an Egyptian name meaning "The Nourisher of the Two Lands, the Living One." This name approximates the consonants of the Hebrew, fits Joseph's accomplishment in planning for the famine, and is roughly similar to several known names from the Old and Middle Kingdoms.[9]

Potiphera and Asenath are not as difficult to deal with. Potiphera is virtually identical with Potiphar, and like the latter is probably a statement of the nationality of the father of Asenath rather than a personal name. He was simply one placed on earth by Re, a "son of Re." Asenath, however, is beyond doubt a proper name, most likely *ns-nt,* "Belonging

7. John Van Seters, *The Hyksos: A New Investigation* (New Haven, CT: Yale University, 1966), pp. 184 – 85.
8. See Kenneth A. Kitchen, "Zaphnath-Paaneah," in *New Bible Dictionary,* ed. J. D. Douglas (Grand Rapids: Eerdmans, 1962), p. 1353, and the extended discussion in Redford, *Study,* pp. 230 – 31.
9. Hermann Ranke, *Die Aegyptische Personennamen* (Glückstadt: J. J. Augustin, 1935), vol. 1, p. 406, nos. 16 – 22.

to [the goddess] Neith." This type of name occurs from the early periods to the later, and is commonly found in the Middle Kingdom.[10]

The title given to Joseph's father-in-law, priest of On, is interesting. On is the Egyptian city *iwnw* (Greek, Heliopolis), the center of worship of the sun god Re. It may be assumed without much doubt that Asenath's father was a high-ranking priest of Re, and therefore one of the leading religious dignitaries of Egypt. He may even have been the high priest,[11] since Joseph's marriage to his daughter was considered to be a great honor. That Joseph's bride was the daughter of a priest of the sun god is an important confirmation of a Middle Kingdom date for these events, since the Hyksos kings (after 1675 B.C.) made Set the primary deity of their rule rather than Re.[12] Had Joseph's pharaoh been a Hyksos, he would most likely have given Joseph a wife from the family of some priest of Set instead of Re.

Joseph as Second Ruler of Egypt

Much study has been given to what titles Joseph had (and did not have) in the Egyptian government. The chief difficulty lies in the fact that for the most part the Hebrew narrative does not preserve translations or transliterations of Egyptian titles, but attempts rather to paraphrase or describe them. And since the functions of Egyptian officials often overlapped, it is hard to determine with precision which title is meant in a given passage of Scripture.

To begin with the most obvious titles, it seems certain that Joseph became chief steward of the king. Genesis 41:40 quotes the pharaoh as saying that Joseph would be over the king's house; in Egyptian usage this meant over his estates and agricultural holdings as well as the royal residence itself. This

10. Ibid., vol. 1, p. 176, no. 14.

11. So Alan Rowe, "The Famous Solar City of On," *Palestine Exploration Quarterly* 94 (1962): 134 — 35.

12. The view that the Hyksos completely suppressed the worship of Re can no longer be accepted. See Van Seters, *Hyksos*, pp. 172 — 73.

appointment is reiterated in the important summary of Joseph's titles in Genesis 45:8, where he is called "lord of all his [pharaoh's] house."

Chief stewards were first and foremost administrators of the king's personal agricultural lands, and had within their jurisdiction the royal slaves who labored upon these lands.[13] This conforms exactly to Joseph's experience in the house of Potiphar, where he had responsibilities over the fields and most certainly over the agricultural laborers. It also conforms to his agriculture-related duties in preparing Egypt for the coming famine, as would his second task as chief steward— superintending the royal granaries. A further task of the chief steward was oversight of the king's cattle and other animals. A reflection of this particular duty is perhaps seen in the pharaoh's offhand question to Joseph in Genesis 47:6, where he asks if any of the children of Israel have special talent in this area. All considered, the agricultural nature of the office of chief steward gave Joseph the opportunity to help save Israel from starvation. Note what he says to his brothers in Genesis 45:7: "And God sent me before you to preserve you a posterity in the earth, and to save your lives by a great deliverance."

Genesis 45:8 also mentions another important Egyptian dignity, calling Joseph "father to Pharaoh." As has been correctly pointed out by William A. Ward, this is the title *father of god*, where the term *god* refers to the king.[14] The title had, like many Egyptian titles, several uses. It could mean the literal father of the king, the father-in-law of the king, the king's private tutor, or it could even be used of minor priestly functionaries. None of these positions of course were held by Joseph. But another very common use of the title was to designate important officials who were unrelated to the king

13. The most complete job description of the office of chief steward is Wolfgang Helck, *Zur Verwaltung des Mittleren und Neuen Reichs* (Leiden: E. J. Brill, 1958), pp. 103 – 04.

14. William A. Ward, "The Egyptian Office of Joseph," *Journal of Semitic Studies* 5 (1960): 149. The title is further discussed in Alan H. Gardiner, *Ancient Egyptian Onomastica* (Oxford: Oxford University, 1947), vol. 1, pp. 47ff.

but had performed some valuable function or held some exalted position.[15] The title was particularly common among viziers, a fact we must remember when we consider whether Joseph was ever prime minister or not.

Ward has seen two other titles in the biblical description of Joseph, seal-bearer of the king, which he assigns on the basis of the mention of the ring in Genesis 41:42, and overseer of the granaries of Upper and Lower Egypt, which he assigns on the basis of the obvious need for grain in preparation for the famine.[16] As for the title seal-bearer, Ward may well be right; there is simply not enough information in the biblical text to conclude the case one way or the other. It is not possible, however, that Joseph was overseer of the granaries, since this title did not appear until the Eighteenth Dynasty, long after the days of Joseph. In the Middle Kingdom responsibility for crop administration fell under the vizier or prime minister.[17] This brings us to the most controversial question regarding Joseph's titles: was he ever vizier of Egypt?

Ward is the strongest advocate of the view that Joseph was never vizier of Egypt. His chief argument is that phrases such as "ruler over all the land" (Gen. 41:43) and "ruler throughout all the land of Egypt" (Gen. 45:8) are merely Hebrew translations of high-sounding but basically meaningless Egyptian epithets given to all important officials.[18] While no one denies that Egyptian officials did have epithets that were, as far as we know, devoid of specific meaning, most of the biblical phrases in question are not exact renditions of the typical airy epithets. The only such common epithet which is applied to Joseph is "chief of the entire land," which was, as Ward points out, sometimes used by officials who were of lesser rank than vizier. Unfortunately for Ward's case, however, the epithet in question was most often used by viziers, and is thus stronger evidence that Joseph held that position than that he did not. Also, for the strongest of all the phar-

---

15. Redford, *Study*, p. 191, has not considered this common use of the title.
16. Ward, "Egyptian Office," pp. 145ff.
17. Helck, *Verwaltung*, p. 154.
18. Ward, "Egyptian Office," pp. 148 – 49.

aoh's statements, "Only in the throne will I be greater than you" (Gen. 41:40), Ward can find no exact Egyptian parallel at all.

It seems far better to accept Genesis 41:40 at face value and assume that Joseph was indeed vizier. In support of this contention, let us briefly compare some of Joseph's responsibilities with the well-known duties of Egyptian viziers.[19] The vizier was indeed the number-two man in all Egypt, directly subordinate to the king. It was his job to supervise the machinery of government at all levels, to keep all administrative records, to appoint lower officials, to receive embassies, and to supervise agriculture, construction work, and industry generally. When we see Joseph preparing Egypt for the coming famine, we see nothing less than an all-powerful vizier at work. Not only was crop management directly under the vizier in the Middle Kingdom, but who else could have carried out such massive land reforms as those mentioned in Genesis 47:20−26? Also, as we have mentioned, the vizier was charged with the reception of foreign embassies, a duty we see Joseph performing when his brothers travel to Egypt in search of food. Finally, the report brought back to Jacob by the brothers that Joseph was governor over all Egypt (Gen. 45:26) is best taken to mean that Joseph was indeed vizier under kings Sesostris II and the great Sesostris III.

In regard to the seven-year famine, let it be said that we have no certain record of this particular catastrophe, which would have fallen during the reign of Sesostris III. But we do have an interesting text from the Ptolemaic period which refers to a famine of seven years' duration and the measures taken to alleviate it; supposedly this event occurred in the reign of King Djoser in the Old Kingdom.[20] This text shows at least that there was some knowledge of a famine lasting seven years; and, further, it is just possible that this text is a garbled Ptolemaic recollection of Joseph's famine and not

19. On the duties of the vizier, see William C. Hayes, *Egypt: Internal Affairs from Tuthmosis I to the Death of Amenophis III* (Cambridge: Cambridge University, 1966), part 1, pp. 43ff.

20. For analysis and bibliography, see Redford, *Study,* pp. 206 − 07.

Egyptian tomb painting.

one in Djoser's day. We must remember that Djoser had a vizier famous for wisdom, the semilegendary Imhotep. It would not be difficult for people living over one thousand years later to attribute Joseph's accomplishments to another famous vizier; we should also consider the fact that the inscription about Djoser's famine was found near the site of a Jewish colony in southern Egypt, thus making reference to Joseph highly possible.[21]

Finally, we must address ourselves to the complex issue of Joseph's land reforms described in Genesis 47:20–26. Although the system of land tenure in Middle Kingdom Egypt is poorly understood, it is clear that in this age, as in all periods of Egyptian history, some private ownership of land continued to exist.[22] But the abolition of private property is perhaps not what is implied in the biblical passage. An im-

21. Ronald J. Williams, "Egypt and Israel," in J. R. Harris, ed., *The Legacy of Egypt* (New York: Oxford University, 1971), p. 271.

22. Redford, *Study*, pp. 236 – 37.

Osiris, god of the nether world.

portant social reform did in fact take place during the very time of Joseph, the reign of Sesostris III. Sesostris broke the dominance of the great nobles of the land. It is noteworthy that in the late years of his reign the records of the nomarchs (provincial chiefs) and the building of impressive tombs for officials in the provinces came to an end.[23] It is probable that there is some link between the decline of the great nobles and Joseph's land reforms,[24] but the details must await further research.

The last verse in the Book of Genesis tells us that Joseph died at 110, and was embalmed and put into a coffin in Egypt. At that time 110 years was considered the ideal life-span,[25] and the embalming of bodies was fast becoming a key part of Egyptian funerary practice.

23. For the details see William C. Hayes, *The Middle Kingdom of Egypt* (New York: Cambridge University, 1964), pp. 44 – 45.

24. So James R. Battenfield, "A Consideration of the Identity of the Pharaoh of Genesis 47," *Journal of the Evangelical Theological Society* 15 (Spring, 1972): 82ff.

25. See the statement at the end of the "Instructions of Ptah-hotep," in Miriam Lichtheim, *Ancient Egyptian Literature*, 2 vols. (Berkeley: University of California, 1973, 1976), vol. 1, p. 76.

The death of Joseph initiated a change in the attitude of the Egyptians toward the resident Hebrews, although the effects of this change were not immediate. But within a century of the reign of Sesostris III, the entire political and social situation in Egypt was to change radically, and with these changes came the oppression of the children of Israel.

4

The Sojourn and Bondage

Egypt After Joseph

The Hyksos

With the end of Dynasty Twelve (ca. 1786 B.C.) the greatness that had characterized the Middle Kingdom had run its course. Under the ephemeral rulers called the Thirteenth Dynasty, Egypt was no longer a great power; and with the decline of central authority came ever increasing infiltration of Asiatics into the delta. Eventually, although the details are obscure and still a matter of scholarly debate,[1] the Asiatics usurped power and established a kingdom of their own in the Nile delta. These Asiatics adopted much of the culture of Egypt, and their pharaohs are known to historians as Dynasties Fifteen and Sixteen, or as the *Hyksos*, a corruption of an Egyptian term meaning "Rulers of Foreign Countries."

Although the period of Hyksos rule (ca. 1675 – 1570 B.C.) is one of the most poorly documented periods of Egyptian history, modern research has shown that some of the old ideas about this age are untrue. The most significant of the misconceptions is that the Hyksos possessed a vast empire in Syria-Palestine and from there sent out their chariots in a

---

1. See John Van Seters, *The Hyksos: A New Investigation* (New Haven, CT: Yale University, 1966), chapter 8, for the latest arguments.

massive and highly organized invasion of Egypt. We now realize that no such attack occurred, nor did the Hyksos have an empire of any kind outside of Egypt. A second wrong idea current in recent years is that the Hyksos ruled all of Egypt. It is now known that they ruled only the northern part of the country; the south remained under the control of native Egyptian rulers. Finally, it has been popular, on the basis of wrong interpretations of Egyptian texts, to see the Hyksos as persecutors of native Egyptian religious beliefs. While it is true that the Hyksos showed preference to certain Egyptian deities (notably Set), they did not actively suppress the worship of any gods as far as we know.

About 1570 B.C. the native rulers at Thebes in Upper Egypt (first the Seventeenth and then the Eighteenth Dynasties) succeeded in expelling the Hyksos from the delta, united the country, and inaugurated Egypt's greatest period of all, the New Kingdom.

Dynasty Eighteen: The Early New Kingdom

Many recent studies have placed our knowledge of the chronology of the Eighteenth Dynasty on a fairly firm footing.[2] There is little likelihood of substantial error in the following list of kings and dates:

Ahmose I	1570 – 1546
Amenhotep I	1546 – 1526
Thutmosis I	1526 – 1518
Thutmosis II	1518 – 1504
Hatshepsut	1504 – 1482
Thutmosis III	1504 – 1450
Amenhotep II	1453 – 1415
Thutmosis IV	1415 – 1401
Amenhotep III	1401 – 1364

2. See Erik Hornung, *Untersuchungen zur Chronologie und Geschichte des Neuen Reichs* (Wiesbaden: Otto Harrassowitz, 1964); or more recently, E. F. Wente and C. Van Sicklen, "A Chronology of the New Kingdom," in *Studies in Honor of George R. Hughes*, ed. Janet H. Johnson, Studies in Ancient Oriental Civilization 39 (Chicago: University of Chicago, 1976), pp. 217 – 61.

Akhenaton	1364 – 1347
Smenkhare	1347 – 1344
Tutankhamon	1344 – 1335
Ay	1335 – 1331
Horemhab	1331 – 1304

Ahmose I, the founder of the Eighteenth Dynasty,[3] was the brother of the last king of the Seventeenth Dynasty, Kamose, and finished the expulsion of the Hyksos begun by his predecessors. After a reign of about twenty-four years, which included a war with Nubia and the crushing of a rebellion at home, Ahmose died and was succeeded by his son Amenhotep I.

The new king finished the consolidation of power begun by his father, campaigning in Nubia again and even repelling a Libyan invasion of the western delta. By the end of his twenty-year reign, it was clear that the Theban Eighteenth Dynasty was securely in control of the land and Egypt was on the threshold of a new golden age in its history.

The death of Amenhotep I created a potential dynastic crisis, for the king had no son. Fortunately, one of Amenhotep's female relatives (either his sister or his daughter) was married to a prominent general, and the crown passed to him as Thutmosis I.

The new king fought two Nubian campaigns, but of greater importance was a deep thrust into Syria-Palestine, penetrating all the way to the upper Euphrates River, where a victory stele was set up in commemoration of the defeat of the local princes. This was the first of many such invasions of Syria-Palestine by the pharaohs of Dynasty Eighteen, the net result of which was the creation of an Asiatic empire for Egypt. That, however, came later; Thutmosis's campaign was in reality only a raid.

After reigning about seven years, Thutmosis died, causing an interesting succession problem. He and his queen had no

3. For the history of Dynasty Eighteen, see George Steindorff and Keith C. Seele, *When Egypt Ruled the East* (Chicago: University of Chicago, 1965).

Hatshepsut's temple at Deir el-Bahri.

son to succeed as pharaoh, but did have a daughter, Hatshepsut. She was, being female, considered unfit to be king, and was therefore compelled to marry her half brother Thutmosis, son of Thutmosis I by a secondary wife. The new king reigned as Thutmosis II for about fourteen years, but was not a talented ruler.

In 1504 B.C., Thutmosis II died; like his father, he had no heir by his queen, Hatshepsut. A son by a secondary wife was named king as Thutmosis III, but since this prince was a mere boy incapable of ruling, the strong-willed Hatshepsut seized the real power and ruled for twenty-two years as virtual king. Thutmosis III was forced into the background during Hatshepsut's dominance.

Hatshepsut was a colorful ruler. She sent a trading expedition to the fabled African land of Punt, which she commemorated by a series of scenes in her beautiful terraced temple built against the cliffs at Deir el-Bahri on the west side of the Nile at Thebes. Aside from these peaceful pursuits, the "Female King" apparently had some warlike inclinations, for there is evidence that Hatshepsut conducted at least four campaigns.[4] In one of these operations she even led the army in person!

After twenty-two years of rule, Hatshepsut disappeared from the scene, whether by a natural death or through foul

4. D. B. Redford, *History and Chronology of the Eighteenth Dynasty of Egypt* (Toronto: University of Toronto, 1967), pp. 62ff.

Pylon at Karnak.

play we cannot tell. Thutmosis III emerged from the shadows to rule as well as reign, becoming perhaps the greatest king Egypt ever had.

If we count back to his coronation, Thutmosis III reigned for fifty-four years; his effective rule began, however, in 1482 B.C. From that year to his death in 1450, Thutmosis campaigned seventeen times, mainly in Syria-Palestine but also in Nubia. The result of these wars was the creation of an Egyptian empire in the Levant, for Thutmosis occupied much of the territory in which he fought.

The booty brought back from Thutmosis's Asiatic wars was immense. Lists of slaves, cattle, and precious metals form the bulk of the king's famous annals inscribed on the walls of the great temple of Amon-Re at Karnak.[5] The fact that these records were placed in a temple rather than a palace bears witness to another significant factor of Thutmosis's reign, the rise in wealth and power of the priesthood of the state god Amon-Re. Much of the wealth taken in war was given to the

5. For these annals, see James H. Breasted, *Ancient Records of Egypt* (Chicago: University of Chicago, 1906), vol. 2, par. 406ff.

Obelisk at Karnak.

god, as the annals show, and further expenditure of state funds was lavished on construction at Karnak and other temples. It was during this age that the priests of Amon reached a position of influence second only to the king himself. The seeds of the religious revolution of Akhenaton were sown.

Late in life, the elderly Thutmosis III raised his son Amenhotep to the kingship, creating a coregency of something approaching three years. In 1450 the old king died, and Amenhotep II began his long sole reign as pharaoh.[6]

6. Previous estimates placed the sole reign of Amenhotep II at about twenty-five years, but it now seems that thirty-five is closer to the truth. See Wente and Van Sicklen, "Chronology," pp. 227ff.

Avenue of Sphinxes at Karnak.

Amenhotep was a true son of his father. We are fortunate to have extant records telling of the king's great athletic and military prowess, particularly in the areas of archery and horsemanship.[7] Despite Amenhotep's interest in things military, however, he has left records of only three major wars, in years three, seven, and nine of his reign.[8] Since the wars of years three and seven are both called the first campaign, D. B. Redford, following Alt, believes that Amenhotep did in fact have two "first" wars: one before the death of Thutmosis III and one after he became sole monarch.[9] If this is true (and it appears very likely), the war of year three took place in 1450, that of year seven in 1446, and that of year nine in 1444. This point will be of interest when we consider the exodus.

Following the uneventful reign of Thutmosis IV (who was

7. *Ancient Near Eastern Texts Relating to the Old Testament*, ed. James B. Pritchard (Princeton, NJ: Princeton University, 1950), pp. 244 – 45.

8. On all of this see D. B. Redford, "The Coregency of Thutmosis III and Amenophis II," *Journal of Egyptian Archaeology* 51 (1965): 118ff.

9. Ibid., p. 120.

Statue of Amenhotep II.

a son of Amenhotep II, but not the firstborn—see p. 104), Amenhotep III sat on Egypt's throne for thirty-eight years. His reign was one of comparative peace and great prosperity, but was also the prelude to the great religious and social upheaval known as the Amarna revolution.

Akhenaton (originally Amenhotep IV), son of Amenho-

Amenhotep II in his chariot. *Courtesy, Howard F. Vos.*

tep III, began to reign at the death of the elder king in 1364 B.C.[10] In the new king's sixth year of rule, Akhenaton and his queen Nefertiti officially abolished the worship of the state god Amon-Re, abandoned Thebes and its established bureaucratic tradition, and set up a new capital on virgin soil at Tell el-Amarna in Middle Egypt. The new state god was the Aton, the raw disk of the sun; a priesthood and dogma were developed to replace those of Amon-Re. The army, evidently supportive of these changes, was called home from Palestine, and Egypt's empire was neglected. The neglect of foreign affairs is clearly revealed in the extensive diplomatic correspondence known as the Amarna Letters which was found

10. The present author does not believe a coregency between Amenhotep III and Akhenaton existed. See Redford, *History and Chronology,* chapter 5, for a full discussion.

Akhenaton and Nefertiti with offerings for the sun-god Aton. *Photograph, Courtesy of The Metropolitan Museum of Art.*

at the capital. In these documents princes and chieftains in Syria-Palestine pleaded for military aid from the pharaoh against attackers, but no help was forthcoming.

One of the great misconceptions commonly held concerning Akhenaton is that he was a monotheist. Such was simply not the case. Not all Egypt's gods were abolished along with Amon-Re, nor did the king deny that he himself was divine. Quite the contrary, Akhenaton became the intermediary deity through whom the common people worshiped the Aton. The people venerated their divine king; he in turn worshiped the new sun god. Another important fact to remember is that Akhenaton most certainly had motives for changing Egypt's religion that were far from religious. The Amon priesthood had become wealthy and too powerful, a rival institution to

Bust of Nefertiti. *Courtesy of the Oriental Institute, University of Chicago. (The photograph depicts an Oriental Institute cast which is a reproduction of the original in the collection of the Egyptian Museum at Charlottenburg Castle in West Berlin.)*

the throne itself. Something drastic had to be done to weaken the priests, and the Amarna revolution was the solution.[11]

Akhenaton's religious beliefs died with him. The last pharaohs of Dynasty Eighteen led a return to the old capital at Thebes and to the old gods as well. Efforts were made to suppress even the memory of the reformer and his religion. The details of the reigns of Smenkhare, Tutankhamon (the boy king whose tomb was found virtually intact), Ay, and Horemhab need not detain us here. These last kings of the dynasty merely stabilized Egypt for the renewal of greatness in Dynasty Nineteen.

11. For details see Charles F. Aling, "A Prosopographical Study of the Reigns of Thutmosis IV and Amenhotep III" (Ph.D. dissertation, University of Minnesota, 1976), chapter 10.

The Bondage

The Length of the Sojourn

The preceding digression from the biblical account is necessary background to our discussion of the sojourn and exodus. Two basic views are held today regarding the length of Israel's stay in Egypt.[12] The first view is that the total length of the sojourn was 215 years. This is based on Galatians 3:16—17, which seemingly places the giving of the law to Moses 430 years after the promises made to Abraham in Genesis 12:1—3. Since these promises (ca. 2091) preceded Jacob's entry into Egypt (ca. 1876) by 215 years, the sojourn in Egypt would have lasted 215 years. A sojourn of only 215 years is seemingly supported by Exodus 6:16—20, which mentions only four generations from Levi to Moses, and by the Septuagint reading of Exodus 12:40, which, in reference to the sojourn, substitutes 215 years for the 430 years of the Hebrew text.

But the primary evidence seems to favor a longer sojourn of 430 years. First and foremost, the Hebrew text asserts that the Israelites spent 430 years in Egypt (Exod. 12:40—41); and, as Leon Wood states, the Hebrew text must be favored over later versions.[13] Second, God told Abraham in Genesis 15:13 that his descendants would be afflicted in a foreign land for four hundred years. Nor need we regard Exodus 6:16—20 as strictly genealogical. This passage probably is meant to give Moses' tribe, clan, and family rather than specific individuals.

The only apparent remaining difficulty with a 430-year sojourn lies with Galatians 3:16—17. But after further examination of that passage, this difficulty passes away. William Hendriksen in his commentary on Galatians puts his finger on the most logical solution: in verse 16 Paul states that the promises were made not only to Abraham but to his seed or descendants as well.[14] Thus, the 430 years could begin with the confirmation of the promises to Jacob (Gen. 28:14), making the sojourn itself 430 years and conforming to the Hebrew reading of Exodus 12:40. It seems best to accept the 430 years

12. These views are treated at length in Leon Wood, *A Survey of Israel's History* (Grand Rapids: Zondervan, 1970), chapter 5.

13. Ibid., pp. 83—84.

14. William Hendriksen, *Galatians* (Grand Rapids: Baker, 1968), pp. 138—39.

in accord with the Hebrew text, and reject the 215 years of the Septuagint.

The Start of the Bondage

It is unlikely that the bondage of the resident Hebrews began as soon as Joseph was dead. There may have been sporadic and isolated cases of persecution against the Jews, but in general the Egyptians must have remembered Joseph and what he had done for their country. Nor would resident Asiatics have been a source of concern to the natives of the land; quite the contrary, the last years of the Middle Kingdom witnessed an increasing influx of Asiatics, most of whom adopted the civilization of their new home. Some, like Joseph, reached positions of authority and even intermarried with Egyptians, despite their original servile status.[15]

Organized persecution began, according to Exodus 1:8, with the rise to power of a new king over Egypt who did not know of Joseph. In his definitive article on the oppression and exodus, John Rea effectively argues that the king who knew not Joseph was one of the Hyksos pharaohs of the Second Intermediate Period.[16] Rea's thesis rests on two points in Scripture and one archaeological factor. First, the Hebrew phrase translated "arose...over Egypt" might better be rendered "arose against Egypt"; in other Old Testament passages the preposition 'al is often used to refer to violent seizures of the throne, but never to peaceful succession of kings. The idea of violent seizure of the throne fits the Hyksos better than any native Egyptian ruler of this period. Second, in Exodus 1:9—10 the oppressing king, in giving his reason for reducing the Hebrews to slavery, states that they have become "more and mightier than we," and he fears they may join with his enemies. It is inconceivable that the Israelites could ever have outnumbered the natives of Egypt, but it is very possible they could have been more numerous than the Hyk-

15. Van Seters, *Hyksos*, p. 90.
16. John Rea, "The Time of the Oppression and the Exodus," *Grace Journal* 2, no. 1 (1961): 6 — 10.

sos ruling minority. On the archaeological side, the biblical statement that the Hebrews labored at the city of Ramses fits the Hyksos Period.

This brings us to one of the most difficult questions regarding the sojourn and bondage. Exodus 1:11 affirms that the Hebrew bondage began at two cities, Pithom and Ramses. Before much can be said concerning these places, we must consider the controversial issue of their exact location. Scholarly debate over the location of Pithom (Egyptian *pr itm*, House of Atum) has narrowed the choice to three possibilities.[17]

1. *Tell el-Maskhutah*. This eleven-acre town, located near the eastern end of the Wadi Tumilat in the northeastern part of the Nile delta, was the choice of the noted Swiss Egyptologist Edouard Naville. His identification was based primarily on two post—New Kingdom inscriptions which make reference to the city as Per Atum,[18] and on the fact that Tell el-Maskhutah is situated on the main route out of Egypt toward Palestine. Unfortunately, the name Per Atum for this city is very late (first used in the reign of Osorkon II, ninth century B.C.), its name in the New Kingdom being Tcheku. Moreover, the location of the city near the eastern frontier (on a potential escape route from Egypt) makes it unlikely that foreign slaves would be stationed there. Most scholars today have abandoned the idea that Tell el-Maskhutah was biblical Pithom.

2. *Tell er-Retaba*. Tell er-Retaba, also located in the Wadi Tumilat but slightly to the west of Maskhutah, is the choice of Alan H. Gardiner and T. Eric Peet, among others.[19] Two points support this identification. First, the evidence linking Maskhutah with Pithom is far from conclusive; in fact, the references to that city as Tcheku cast strong doubt on its being Pithom, since many scholars equate Tcheku with bib-

---

17. For all the arguments see E. P. Uphill, "Pithom and Ramses: Their Location and Significance," *Journal of Near Eastern Studies* 27, no. 4 (1968): 291 — 99.

18. Ibid., p. 294.

19. For a summary of the arguments, see T. Eric Peet, *Egypt and the Old Testament* (Liverpool: University of Liverpool, 1924), pp. 67ff.

EGYPT, the Eastern Delta Region

lical Succoth, which was east of Pithom. Second, Retaba had a temple of Atum, and could thus qualify as the "House of Atum," that is, Pithom.

3. *Heliopolis.* E. P. Uphill, writing in 1968, made an appealing case for the equation of Heliopolis (Egyptian *iwnw*, Hebrew On) with Pithom.[20] He points out that this city above all others in Egypt was the center of solar worship (Atum was a sun god), and even had temples known as Per Re (House of Re) and Per Atum (House of Atum). Nor in the case

20. Uphill, "Pithom and Ramses," pp. 296ff.

of Heliopolis is there any problem with the date. Heliopolis was the center of the cults of Re and Atum as early as the Old Kingdom.

Of the three possibilities, Tell er-Retaba and Heliopolis seem to be the only viable choices for biblical Pithom. All that can be said with certainty at present is that Pithom was in northern Egypt and probably is to be identified with one of the great centers of solar worship.

With Ramses, originally known as Avaris, we are on firmer ground thanks to recent textual research and excavations. Until recently, the one-thousand-acre delta city of Tanis (biblical Zoan) had been identified with Ramses, chiefly on the basis of the many statues and other monuments of the Nineteenth-Dynasty king Ramses II (1290 – 1223 B.C.) found there, some of which even carry inscriptions referring to deities "of Ramses" (the city, not the king).[21] But several facts can be cited against this identification: (1) In order to have been Avaris-Ramses, Tanis must have been a major city in two periods, the Nineteenth Dynasty (the dynasty of Ramses II) and the Hyksos Period, when Ramses, known as Avaris, was the capital of northern Egypt. And yet Tanis yields no small everyday finds from these periods; its earliest large-scale habitation began only with Dynasty Twenty-one.[22] (2) Of the objects found at Tanis bearing the name of Ramses II, not one was found in a building constructed during his reign. On the contrary, they were haphazardly scattered about, and those blocks with King Ramses's name on them were clearly reused as building material by later rulers.[23] Ramesside objects were thus brought here by the kings of Dynasty Twenty-one. There is no evidence of earlier building at Tanis. (3) In a well-known list of cities from the Nineteenth Dynasty, Tanis and Ramses are both mentioned—and are separated by the names of several other cities.[24] They are clearly different places.

If Tanis was not Ramses, where was the biblical city? Ex-

---

21. See the list in Uphill, "Pithom and Ramses," pp. 305 – 06.
22. Van Seters, *Hyksos*, p. 131.
23. Ibid., pp. 130ff., and Uphill, "Pithom and Ramses," pp. 307 – 08.
24. Uphill, "Pithom and Ramses," p. 307.

citing new archaeological evidence has come to light, supported by the sound study of previously known textual material, which shows beyond serious doubt that Avaris-Ramses was located in the Khatana-Qantir Tell ed-Daba area in the eastern delta, south of Tanis.[25] There are several pieces of supporting evidence: (1) Small finds from the days of Ramses II abound in the Qantir area. Particularly impressive are the many glazed blue tiles for use in a royal palace, some of which name Ramses II and others Seti I (the father of Ramses). In the same area there was a factory for the manufacture of these tiles, with ten thousand tile molds of eight hundred different types. (2) Qantir also has provided numerous small finds (mostly pottery) from the Hyksos Period and even the earlier Middle Kingdom. Unlike Tanis, this city was obviously a large habitation site in times earlier than Dynasty Twenty-one or Dynasty Nineteen. (3) Qantir's location, buildings, and gods correspond with all that we know of Per Ramses (Egyptian, "House [or city] of Ramses") from Egyptian literary sources. (4) Ostraca have been found north of the tile factory which actually bear the name Per Ramses.

The case for Khatana-Qantir Tell ed-Daba being Per Ramses seems conclusive. The identification is supported by such notables in the field of Egyptology as Mahmud Hamza and Labib Habachi, both experts on the archaeology of the delta. This identification permits us to date the start of the bondage in the Hyksos Period, for Qantir thrived as early as the Middle Kingdom.

The Height of the Bondage

We are informed in Exodus 1:13–14 that as time passed, the labor of the Hebrews was heightened and extended. They worked in mortar and brick as well as in all types of agricultural labor. We may conclude from this that their service spread geographically too, away from the cities of Pithom and Ramses. The identity of those who heightened the bond-

25. For a summary of the arguments see Van Seters, *Hyksos*, pp. 132ff., and especially Uphill, "Pithom and Ramses," pp. 308ff.

age is also told us (v. 13): it was the native Egyptians themselves, not the Hyksos. Here we are probably to recognize the early pharaohs of the Eighteenth Dynasty, as John Davis has recently suggested.[26] It is likely that the king of verse 15 who ordered the Hebrew midwives to kill Israelite male infants was Thutmosis I, although this cannot be stated with certainty.

In regard to the materials mentioned in verse 14, mortar and brick, a number of interesting points may be raised. By mortar (or clay, Hebrew *hōmer*) we are not to understand that some form of modern cementing material was used; nothing of the kind was known in the ancient world before Greco-Roman times. In brick construction work (which comprised the majority of all architecture in ancient Egypt) the sandy Nile clay was used as an adhesive. It was ideal for this purpose.[27] The bricks mentioned were certainly the common Egyptian sun-dried bricks, the normal building material in the timberless Nile Valley. Incidentally, the purpose of chopped straw in Egyptian brickmaking was to strengthen the brick and to increase its moldability.

Kenneth Kitchen's recent discussion of brickmaking in Egypt sheds light on some of the details in Exodus 1–5.[28] From Egyptian texts we learn that a dual administration existed for brickmaking, consisting of Egyptian supervisors holding authority over foremen (cf. Exod. 5:6). Also, production quotas, down to the last brick, were set.

As a final note on the making of bricks by the Hebrews, there is a famous painting at Thebes in the tomb of Rekhmire, vizier under the great Pharaoh Thutmosis III, which depicts foreign slaves (both Nubians and light-skinned Syrians) making bricks.[29] Since the exodus followed shortly after the death

26. John J. Davis, *Moses and the Gods of Egypt* (Grand Rapids: Baker, 1971), p. 49.

27. See A. Lucas and J. R. Harris, *Ancient Egyptian Materials and Industries* (London: Edward Arnold, 1962), pp. 74 – 75.

28. Kenneth A. Kitchen, "From the Brickfields of Egypt," *Tyndale Bulletin* 27 (1976): 137 – 47.

29. See the discussion of this scene in Norman de Garis Davies, *The Tomb of Rekh-mi-Re at Thebes*, Metropolitan Museum of Art Egyptian Expedition Publications 11 (New York: Arno Press, 1973 reprint), pp. 54 – 55.

Brickmaking in Eighteenth-Dynasty Egypt (from the tomb of Rekhmire). *Ph* *ography by the Egyptian Exhibition, The Metropolitan Museum of Art.*

of Thutmosis III (see chapter 5), this scene must depict the last difficult days of the bondage. It is the only depiction of brickmaking in all of the hundreds of tomb paintings from the New Kingdom.

The Rise of Moses

Moses, the man chosen by God to deliver the Israelites from their bondage, was born about 1526 B.C. at the end of the reign of Amenhotep I.[30] The account of his being placed in an ark in the Nile by his mother and the discovery of that ark by the pharaoh's daughter is familiar to all of us. The infant was named Moses by the Egyptian princess after he was taken from the water. It is only natural that the pharaoh's daughter would select an Egyptian name familiar to her; and in fact *Moshe* (Hebrew) corresponds (with one consonantal

30. This is deduced from the fact that he was eighty at the time of the exodus, which took place in about 1446 B.C. See chapter 5.

change, *s* to *š*)[31] to the common Egyptian root *ms*, meaning "to give birth." In Egyptian names *ms* was often combined with the pronoun *sw* (him) and the name of a deity, yielding "the god X bore him." Typical examples abound, including the well-known names Ramses and Amenmeses, translated "Ra [Re] is the one who bore him" and "Amon is the one who bore him."

The question might be asked how viewing Moses as a name like Ramses or Amenmeses can be squared with the statement of Exodus 2:10 that the infant was called Moses by the pharaoh's daughter because she drew him out of the water. It is to be noted that the name of any Egyptian deity could be prefixed to the phrase *ms-sw*—we need not see in the name Moses a shortening of either Ramses or Amenmeses. For obvious religious reasons we may assume Moses dropped the pagan deity's name upon identifying himself with the Hebrew people and their God. When the pharaoh's daughter named the child drawn from the waters of the Nile, she may well have selected one of the deities associated with that river, such as Hapi or Osiris. Names compounded with Hapi abounded in the New Kingdom,[32] as did names in which Osiris is an element.[33] The actual name Osiris-meses is even attested, although from a later period than the days of Moses.[34] It seems likely that some such name as Hapi-meses or Osiris-meses was given to Moses. Thus the pharaoh's daughter would have named the child something like "the Nile god bore him" because she drew him out of the water.

It is sometimes stated that Hatshepsut, the daughter of Thutmosis I, is the princess spoken of in the Book of Exodus.[35] While such an identification is tempting in the light of Hatshepsut's domineering personality and her later ac-

---

31. For an explanation of the consonantal change see J. Gwyn Griffiths, "The Egyptian Derivation of the Name Moses," *Journal of Near Eastern Studies* 12 (1953): 225 – 31.

32. Hermann Ranke, *Die Aegyptische Personennamen* (Glückstadt: J. J. Augustin, 1935), vol. 1, p. 234, nos. 8 – 9.

33. Ibid., pp. 84 – 85, nos. 21ff.

34. Ibid., p. 84, no. 26.

35. Wood, *Survey*, pp. 117ff. See Davis, *Moses*, p. 52, n. 19, for further references.

complishments as a female king, we should not place too much stock in such a theory. We must remember that the kings of Egypt often had dozens of daughters, born of their many concubines as well as of the queen herself.

A further reason for caution is the young age of Hatshepsut at the time of Moses' birth (ca. 1526 B.C.). According to the chronology espoused here, Moses was born in the last year of the reign of Amenhotep I or possibly at the start of the reign of Thutmosis I. Thus, as the daughter of Thutmosis I, Hatshepsut was probably very young at the time of Moses' birth. Even though Thutmosis I had married a sister or daughter of Amenhotep I well before the death of the old king,[36] it is difficult to think of Hatshepsut's being old enough in the first year of her father's reign to adopt a son.[37] We must, in view of these difficulties, exercise care in our theories regarding the identity of the pharaoh's daughter, however attractive an identification with the famous Hatshepsut may be.

The first forty years of Moses' life (extending from the reign of Thutmosis I to the last years of the joint rule of Hatshepsut and Thutmosis III) were spent at the Egyptian court, where he received the best education of the day (Acts 7:22). It is worth taking time to investigate the education of a prince in the New Kingdom, since this education prepared Moses for the two great tasks of his life, the leading of Israel out of Egypt and the writing of the Pentateuch.

Teachers were selected not from a class of professional scholars but from among the officials of the land who were favorites of the reigning king.[38] In some cases these were military men; sometimes they were civil officials, like the great chief steward Senmut, tutor of Hatshepsut's daughter. The

36. For the evidence see Alan H. Gardiner, *Egypt of the Pharaohs: An Introduction* (New York: Oxford University, 1966), pp. 177–78.

37. Little is known about Hatshepsut's age at the start of her reign or at her death.

38. Hellmut Brunner, *Altaegyptische Erziehung* (Wiesbaden: Otto Harrassowitz, 1957), pp. 32–33.

subjects taught may be placed into two categories: academic subjects and physical education.

Instruction naturally began with reading and writing.[39] The student was trained in both the hieroglyphic and the hieratic scripts, spending endless hours in copying and memorizing voluminous lists of words and names. The student was also expected to study foreign languages of the Near Eastern world. This doubtless included Akkadian (the language of Babylonia) and the Canaanite dialects necessary for dealing with the peoples of Syria-Palestine. Some mathematics was included, and perhaps a little music. A last academic subject considered of primary importance was rhetoric. The Egyptians highly valued the ability to speak well in public, and accordingly it received heavy attention during the years of formal education. Rhetoric in Egypt comprised not only public speaking but also proper style in writing. Moses certainly put his skills in these last areas to good use, first as a speaker before the pharaoh and before his own people, and second as the writer of the first five books of the Bible.

In the areas of physical training, Egyptian court education was equally rigorous. It included, of course, sports but also military training, again something useful for Moses in his role as leader of the new nation of Israel. The two major military skills taught were chariot driving and archery, but we may assume that the handling of other weapons was also included. The sons of Egyptian kings were encouraged to model themselves after the pattern of the ideal warrior.

It is sometimes asked if a foreigner could in fact be educated at the royal court, and the answer is an emphatic yes. It was common practice in the days of the Egyptian empire to educate the sons of Syrian kings in the Egyptian court. Moses would fit in with such students easily.

It was also possible for foreigners to gain high positions in the New Kingdom.[40] Two of the best-known examples are

---

39. The description of education is drawn from Brunner, *Erziehung,* pp. 98ff.

40. See the excellent discussion in Kenneth A. Kitchen, "Moses," in *New Bible Dictionary,* ed. J. D. Douglas (Grand Rapids: Eerdmans, 1962), pp. 844 – 45.

Hekareshu and his son Hekerneheh, who served under Thutmosis IV and his predecessor Amenhotep II.[41] The father probably made his reputation in the army, and then served in the very responsible position of tutor to the king's sons. Hekerneheh was himself raised at court and ultimately succeeded his father as tutor of the royal princes. Late in life he was also given a high rank in the military, commander of the chariotry. The careers of these two foreigners illustrate that Moses' position at court need not be considered unique.

Because of the great number of royal children born to the rulers of the Eighteenth Dynasty, it is useless to speculate about how high Moses could have risen. It seems rather doubtful that he was in line for the throne; there were certainly other individuals with better claim than he. In any case, Moses forsook his position at court when he fled the country after killing an Egyptian taskmaster. This event occurred when Thutmosis III was ruling jointly with Hatshepsut. The return of Moses after forty years in the wilderness took place after the death of Thutmosis III (Exod. 4:19), during the early years of Amenhotep II. The following chapter will focus on chronological details.

41. For full information see Aling, "Prosopographical Study," pp. 149ff.

5

The Exodus

The Date

There is perhaps no single problem in Hebrew history which has been contested as long or as hotly as the question of the date of the exodus. The exodus itself is important because it lies at the heart of Israel's history, the time when national Israel was born; its date is central to scriptural chronology. This key biblical problem has drawn the interest and labors of scholars in many areas, including Hebrew, cuneiform, Egyptian philology, Near Eastern history, and archaeology. These specialists have raised as many questions as they have answered, and the central issues are by no means solved to everyone's satisfaction. It is not our purpose to describe in full the history of the problem of the date of the exodus;[1] such a task would be far too complex and would need more space than is available here. We will, however, survey the major positions on this issue held by twentieth-century scholars, and present what we believe to be sound arguments for the so-called early date.

1. For an early summary of scholarly opinion see H. H. Rowley, "Israel's Sojourn in Egypt," *Bulletin of the John Rylands Library* 22 (1936): 243 – 90; or G. Ernest Wright, "The Epic of Conquest," *Biblical Archaeologist* 3 (1940): 25 – 40. The most recent summary, with additional bibliography, appears in John J. Bimson, *Redating the Exodus and Conquest,* Journal for the Study of the Old Testament 5 (Sheffield, 1978), pp. 15ff.

The Primary Data

The Key Biblical Passages

There are three biblical references which bear directly on the date of the exodus:

1. I Kings 6:1 states categorically that the start of Solomon's construction of the temple in the fourth year of his reign (966 B.C.) followed the exodus by 480 years. Simple addition gives us 1446 (give or take a year) for the exodus.

2. The period from the start of the conquest of Canaan to the days of Jephthah is given in Judges 11:26 as 300 years. Jephthah judged Israel in about 1100 B.C.;[2] adding 300 to 1100, we arrive at 1400 B.C. for the start of the conquest, and consequently at a date in the fifteenth century for the exodus.

3. Exodus 1:11 deals with the bondage, stating that the Hebrews labored at two cities, Pithom and Ramses. The mention of Ramses is a main pillar of the theory that the exodus took place far later than the fifteenth century, for King Ramses II, the king after whom the city was named, did not reign until the thirteenth century. Thus it is held by many, including some conservatives,[3] that Israel was still in bondage in the 1200s and entered the Promised Land some two hundred years later than what the Bible would seem to indicate in the other two passages.

Extrabiblical Information

There is no direct mention of the Hebrews in bondage, the plagues, the exodus, or the conquest, in any Near Eastern literature outside of the Bible; but this does not mean that there is nothing pertinent in the ancient literature. We should not expect to find records of these events, for Near Eastern peoples were slow to acknowledge defeats, and the exodus and the accompanying occurrences certainly were defeats.

2. For details see Leon Wood, *A Survey of Israel's History* (Grand Rapids: Zondervan, 1970), pp. 89ff.

3. So Kenneth A. Kitchen, *Ancient Orient and Old Testament* (Downers Grove, IL: Inter-Varsity, 1966), pp. 57ff.

Nor can we expect much to be written about slaves. We must remember that such people were chattels, and any mention of them would be purely incidental and as brief as possible.

On the other hand, the corpus of preserved historical records from Egypt and other Near Eastern lands does provide some hints regarding the date of the exodus. We will have occasion to refer to several documents in the course of our discussion; for now, we will cite only the so-called Israel Stele of Merneptah,[4] the Nineteenth-Dynasty king who succeeded Ramses II in 1223 B.C.

The Israel Stele was inscribed and erected after Merneptah expelled an army of Libyan invaders from the Nile delta about 1218 B.C. Although it is a poetic hymn and not a detailed historical account, and attempts to show the pharaoh as a universally triumphant warrior, the Israel Stele does refer to some specific foreign campaigns. Near the end of the text there appears a list of cities and nations subdued by Merneptah, and this list contains the only known reference to Israel in all Egyptian texts:

> The princes are prostrate, saying Mercy! Not one raises his head among the Nine Bows. Desolation is for Tehenu; Hatti is pacified; plundered is the Canaan with every evil; carried off is Ashkelon; seized upon is Gezer; Yenoam is made as that which does not exist; Israel is laid waste, his seed is not; Hurru is become a widow for Egypt! All lands together, they are pacified....[5]

The importance of this reference to Israel is not the assertion that Merneptah defeated the Hebrews, but the fact that he listed them as a nation along with other Palestinian peoples. This demonstrates that Israel was already established in Palestine by about 1220 B.C., and has great implications for the question of the date of the exodus. We will

---

4. For a translation of and commentary on the stele see *Ancient Near Eastern Texts Relating to the Old Testament*, ed. James B. Pritchard (Princeton, NJ: Princeton University, 1950), pp. 376ff.

5. Ibid., p. 378.

return to this point later; here we use it merely to illustrate the bearing that nonbiblical textual material can have on our subject.

Turning from literary evidence to archaeological materials, we note that there is no clear proof of the Hebrew sojourn or of the exodus in Egyptian archaeology. Therefore we must turn to Palestine and attempt to ascertain the date of the conquest, which followed the exodus by forty years. If we can date the conquest, we can also date the exodus.

Archaeology in the last century has done wonders to unfold the history, layer by layer, of Palestine's cities. Names such as Jericho, Lachish, and Hazor have become commonplace to those of us reading archaeological literature. It must be remembered, however, that archaeology is not an exact science; disagreements among the experts occur as a matter of course over how to interpret what has been found. Further, and this is an important point, even if archaeologists discover that a certain city was violently destroyed and come to a tentative agreement on the date of its destruction, there still remains the matter of deciding who destroyed the town. We will have occasion to examine several examples of this type of problem regarding the Israelite conquest. We must keep in mind that, contrary to popular opinion, archaeology has not provided concrete evidence for dating the conquest and the exodus.

The History of the Problem
in the Twentieth Century

Although many dates have been suggested for the exodus, we will restrict our discussion here to four major positions held by segments of the twentieth-century scholarly community:

1. The extreme late date: 1220 B.C. This position became popular after 1911, when it was endorsed by W. M. F. Petrie.
2. The early date: 1446 B.C. Publication of J. W. Jack's *Date of*

the Exodus resulted in increased support for this theory during the 1920s.

3. The extreme early date: 1470 B.C. This view was first propounded in 1978 by John J. Bimson.
4. The late date: 1280 B.C. We will reserve our discussion of this theory until last because it is the most widely held today. It received major impetus beginning in the 1930s from the work of William Foxwell Albright.

The Extreme Late Date: 1220 B.C.

The theory placing the oppression in the days of Ramses II and the exodus in the reign of his successor Merneptah, although originating in the nineteenth century, reached its highest popularity after 1911, when it received the support of W. M. F. Petrie, one of the greatest excavators of his day.[6] This view of the exodus rests on one major argument: since the Hebrews labored in the city of Ramses, the bondage must necessarily have fallen during the reign of Ramses II (1290 – 1223 B.C.), after whom the city was named. The exodus followed Ramses's death, occurring in the early years of Merneptah's reign. If we allow 430 years for the sojourn (Exod. 12:40), Joseph and the start of Israel's residence in Egypt are to be dated in the seventeenth century B.C., during the time of the Hyksos domination.

The extreme late date has three glaring problems:

1. I Kings 6:1, as we have seen, states that the exodus occurred 480 years before Solomon's fourth year, thus in about 1446 B.C. This is in blatant contradiction to Petrie's espousal of 1220 as the date of the exodus.

2. We have argued that Joseph belongs in the Middle Kingdom (pp. 21, 29). Even if we ignore the chronological data given in Scripture, the life of Joseph fits better in the Middle Kingdom than in the Second Intermediate Period. A few examples will make this quite clear.

Joseph is stated to have ruled over all the land of Egypt

6. Cf. W. M. F. Petrie, *Egypt and Israel* (London: Society for Promoting Christian Knowledge, 1911), chapter 3.

(Gen. 45:8). This precludes his serving as vizier under a Hyksos king because the Hyksos never controlled all of Egypt. Further, Joseph's first master was Potiphar, who is specifically called an Egyptian and a commander of the king's guards (Gen. 39:1). It does not seem likely that a foreign king would entrust his personal safety to one of the natives of a subjugated land. Nor would a Hyksos pharaoh have rewarded Joseph by marrying him to the daughter of a priest of the sun god; a Hyksos king would probably have chosen the daughter of the high priest of Set, the favorite god of the Hyksos. Finally, the general details of the story of Joseph fit far better in a period of native rule than in a time of foreign domination.

Dating Joseph to the Hyksos period is based on two arguments, both weak and inconclusive. The first is that since Joseph was a fellow Asiatic, it is likely that it was the Hyksos who elevated him to prominence. This argument is pure supposition, and is not based on any evidence whatsoever; in fact, it contradicts the biblical material cited above. Second, if we start with the presupposition that the exodus occurred in about 1220 B.C., dating Joseph to the Second Intermediate Period accords with Exodus 12:40, which allows 430 years for the sojourn. Adding 430 to 1220 yields a date in the seventeenth century for Joseph. But it is inconsistent to accept Exodus 12:40 at face value while totally rejecting I Kings 6:1. If we accept one of these chronological references, why not accept both?

There is no good reason to assign Joseph to the days of the Hyksos; on the other hand, there are many good reasons, including both biblical chronological references and the background details of the story of Joseph,[7] to date the start of the sojourn two centuries earlier, in the days of the Twelfth Dynasty.

3. The Israel Stele of Merneptah is a major stumbling block for the extreme late date. How could the exodus have taken place as late as 1220 when Merneptah was able to name Israel as a Palestinian nation a scant two years later, in 1218

7. See chapters 2 and 3.

B.C.? There is no room for the forty years in the wilderness and the period of conquest described in the Book of Joshua.

Efforts by scholars to reconcile the Israel Stele with the extreme late date have not been convincing.[8] This point has, except for a small minority of scholars, led to a decrease in the popularity of the position made so attractive by Petrie.

The Early Date: 1446 B.C.

In the 1920s another theory became popular, which dated the exodus to about 1446 B.C. This position, which we shall call the early date for the exodus, originated at an earlier time but became widely held only after the publication of J. W. Jack's *Date of the Exodus* in 1925.[9] The early date is based primarily on a literal acceptance of I Kings 6:1, which places the exodus 480 years before Solomon's fourth year. Jack also stressed the political condition of Syria-Palestine in about 1400 B.C., where, according to information contained in the diplomatic archives known as the Amarna Letters, a people called the Habiru were causing trouble by assaulting cities. Pharaoh Akhenaton paid little heed to the pleas of the Palestinian vassal kings for military assistance, allowing the Habiru to raid the cities unmolested. Proponents of the early date found it hard to resist the temptation to equate the Habiru of the Amarna Letters with the biblical Hebrews under Joshua. After all, here was evidence that a group of raiders were attacking Palestinian cities at about the right time, and

---

8. A typical view is espoused by J. G. Duncan, *New Light on Hebrew Origins* (Naperville, IL: Alec R. Allenson, 1936), namely, that Merneptah defeated the Israelites while they were wandering in the wilderness; this makes no sense in the light of the evidence that Merneptah did in fact capture cities in Palestine. W. F. Albright's proposed proof that Israel was still wandering when beaten by Merneptah (*From the Stone Age to Christianity* [Garden City, NY: Doubleday, 1957], pp. 255 – 56) is without foundation. He argues that the determinative used with the word *Israel* is the determinative used for a people and not for a land. Unfortunately, the Egyptians were not consistent in their use of determinatives. And even if this were an indication that Israel was a relatively new nation on the Palestinian scene, we have no way of knowing how new. The conservative Egyptians were very slow to change the way in which they wrote words.

9. J. W. Jack, *The Date of the Exodus* (Edinburgh: T. and T. Clark, 1925).

even the name of the attackers appeared to be similar to the word *Hebrews* (see p. 109).

In regard to the bondage at Pithom and Ramses, Jack asserted that the city of Ramses could well have been built far earlier than the reign of Ramses II, with that king merely changing the name to reflect his own greatness and building operations there.[10] Thus, the reference in Exodus 1:11 may mean only that the Hebrews served at a city which was later renamed Ramses; they did not necessarily labor under King Ramses II. Modern archaeological work in the Khatana-Qantir area has shown Jack's first assumption to have been correct. Avaris-Ramses was not a new foundation of Ramses II, but existed as a city at least as far back as the Middle Kingdom, thus allowing a Hebrew bondage under the Hyksos.

For a short period of time Jack's theory held the field. But serious archaeological work in Palestine, beginning in the 1930s, discovered what appeared to be a vital flaw in his viewpoint, and turned the tide against him. The cities of Palestine conquered by the incoming Hebrews seemed to yield a unanimous verdict for a later exodus, since many of them were burned in the last quarter of the thirteenth century or later, and not in the fifteenth or early fourteenth centuries. Nor was this all. Scholars began to disassociate the terms *Hebrew* and *Habiru*, showing that they were in all probability not linguistically equatable, and showing that the Habiru activity as recorded in the Amarna Letters was in no way identical with the conquest described in the Bible. By the mid-1930s most scholars had abandoned Jack's early date and had accepted a new thesis which still holds the field today, the late date for the exodus.

The Extreme Early Date: 1470 B.C.

John J. Bimson, in his study *Redating the Exodus and Conquest* (1978), has put forward a new thesis regarding the exodus, dating it to about 1470 B.C. This view is based on archaeological evidence of the destruction of the cities of

10. Ibid., p. 31.

Palestine at the end of the Middle Bronze Age. The view held by many scholars today is that the Hebrew conquest occurred in the Late Bronze Age, but Bimson prefers to equate the widespread destruction at the end of the Middle Bronze Age with the Hebrew attacks. Traditionally, the Middle Bronze Age is thought to have ended about 1550 B.C., and the vast destruction which marks its end is thought to be connected with the expulsion of the Hyksos from Egypt.[11] Bimson, however, lowers the date of the end of the Middle Bronze Age from 1550 to about 1450. He bases his redating on his study of a type of pottery called bichrome ware, which appeared in Palestine at the end of the Middle Bronze Age or at the start of the Late Bronze Age. Bichrome ware has traditionally been associated with the Hyksos, and its appearance in Palestine has thus been thought to coincide with their expulsion from the Nile Valley shortly before 1550 B.C. Bimson points out, correctly, that bichrome ware in Egypt (and in other places as well) has no relation whatever to the Hyksos; in fact, it is found in mid–Eighteenth Dynasty contexts in Egypt.[12] Thus, its introduction into Palestine, and hence the transition from the Middle to the Late Bronze Age, should be dated about 1450 B.C.

If the destruction of the cities of Palestine at the end of the Middle Bronze Age occurred as late as 1450, the conventional view linking their destruction with the expulsion of the Hyksos must be abandoned. Bimson proposes that the destructions were the work of the Hebrews in about 1430 B.C. Adding forty years for the wandering in the wilderness, he arrives at a date of 1470 B.C. for the exodus itself.

There are three difficulties with the view of Bimson:

1. Bimson does not accept I Kings 6:1 literally, but states that he is "assuming that I Kings 6:1 provides only a rough guide to the time of the Exodus, not a precise indication."[13] His rejection of 480 years as the length of time between Solomon's fourth year and the exodus is defended by reference

11. Bimson, *Redating*, pp. 116 – 17.
12. Ibid., pp. 167ff.
13. Ibid., p. 102.

to the as yet poorly understood chronological information given in the Book of Judges, which appears to yield more than 480 years for this period.

2. Assuming with Bimson that the destruction of Palestine's cities at the end of the Middle Bronze Age occurred in about 1450 rather than 1550 B.C., the most logical conclusion is that the destroyers were the energetic conquering pharaohs of the middle Eighteenth Dynasty, and not the Hebrews. The most obvious case in point is Megiddo.

Bimson states that since Egyptian records speak of a seven-month siege of Megiddo by Thutmosis III during his first campaign, but make no specific mention of the destruction of the city, we may conclude that the city was besieged but not destroyed by the Egyptians.[14] Such a view regarding Megiddo seems unrealistic. The logical conclusion of a seven-month siege ending with massive booty for Egypt would be the destruction of the city involved. Regarding the other cities of Palestine, are we to assume that none of them were destroyed in the seventeen Asiatic campaigns of Thutmosis III, not to mention the wars of Thutmosis I and Amenhotep II? The very nature of ancient warfare makes this extremely unlikely. Further, the character of the annals of Thutmosis III makes any reference to specific acts of destruction unlikely. The annals are in the main tribute lists, and not detailed records of the tactical maneuvers of the Egyptian army. Even when pitched battles were fought, we are told little or nothing of their details. The military scribes were mainly interested in the booty. We must also remember that the annals, in their present form on the temple walls at Karnak, were not even exact copies of the military journals, but were refined editions made by temple scribes, men who were even more concerned with spoils as opposed to tactics than were the military scribes in the field.

Since we know the Egyptians were very active militarily in Syria-Palestine in the mid-fifteenth century B.C., it seems best

14. Ibid., p. 154.

to view the destruction of cities in that period as the work of the pharaohs.

3. Another stumbling block to Bimson's view involves the method of capture of Palestinian cities by the Hebrews. In the violent destructions at the end of the Middle Bronze Age burning was a regular feature. The Bible clearly states, however, that after the burning of Jericho and Ai, only Hazor was burned by the Hebrews (Josh. 11:13). Bimson's interpretation that this refers only to northern cities is without support and is unconvincing.[15]

The Late Date: 1280 B.C.

By far the most important scholar in the formulation of the late-date theory of the exodus was the great American archaeologist William Foxwell Albright. Beginning in the mid-1930s, Albright, basing his views on his own field work and reinterpretation of the conclusions of other excavators, theorized that the main thrust of the Hebrew conquest came not around 1400 B.C. but later, at the end of the thirteenth or during the first half of the twelfth century.[16] At Lachish, Bethel, and Tell Beit Mirsim (as well as other places) Albright found evidence of burning and general destruction dating to a period well after the early fourteenth century.[17] One city, however, fell not in the thirteenth or twelfth centuries, but earlier, perhaps in the mid-fourteenth century—Jericho. This led Albright to propose two separate exoduses, one early (reflected in the Amarna references to the Habiru, who Albright said were Hebrews), and one late, under Moses. The later exodus is the one described in the Bible, and Albright dated it to about 1280 B.C. As the years passed, Albright and his numerous followers tended to deemphasize the first exodus and to stress the later one.

15. Ibid., p. 277. In the light of Bimson's theory that the lack of specific records of destruction means that the Egyptians rarely destroyed cities, his statement that "we should not assume that a conquered city was not burned simply because the narrative does not specifically record the fact" is curious.

16. For a summary of his conclusions see Albright, *Stone Age*, pp. 254ff.

17. For discussion and bibliography see John Bright, *A History of Israel*, 2nd ed. (Philadelphia: Westminster, 1972), pp. 126ff.

There are four major reasons why the late date is the one most commonly held by scholars today:

1. The archaeological evidence from Palestine (according to Albright and his supporters) seemingly dates the conquest much later than 1400 – 1350 B.C.; that is, in the last quarter of the thirteenth or the first half of the twelfth century B.C. Many of the cities associated with the Hebrew conquest show clear evidence of burning in the later period, but not in 1400 B.C.[18]

2. Exodus 1:11 states that the Israelites did construction work at the city of Ramses. Since the city was named after King Ramses II (1290 – 1223 B.C.), it is thought that the Hebrews must still have been in Egypt during at least some part of that pharaoh's reign.

3. The biblical accounts of Moses before the pharaoh seemingly imply that these audiences took place near the area where the majority of the Hebrews lived, the land of Goshen in the Nile delta. It is argued by supporters of the late date that the Eighteenth-Dynasty pharaohs had no delta residence, and that it was not until the Nineteenth Dynasty that Egyptian kings of the New Kingdom established a northern capital within easy traveling distance of Goshen.

4. In Numbers 20–21 we learn that Israel was denied passage through the territory of the Edomites and the Amorites. Nelson Glueck, after extensive surface exploration of the Transjordan region, concluded that no sedentary kings resided there until 1300 B.C.[19] Thus, according to the proponents of the late date for the exodus, the episodes involving the Edomites and Amorites could not have taken place in about 1400 B.C., but reflect a later period.

---

18. See, for a sampling of the evidence, W. F. Albright, "Archaeology and the Date of the Hebrew Conquest," *Bulletin of the American Schools of Oriental Research* 58 (April, 1935): 10-18; "Further Light on the History of Israel from Lachish and Megiddo," *BASOR* 68 (December, 1937): 22-26; and "The Israelite Conquest of Canaan in the Light of Archaeology," *BASOR* 74 (April, 1939): 11-23. Albright's views have been adopted by such experts in biblical archaeology and history as G. Ernest Wright, John Bright, and Jack Finegan.

19. Full discussion and bibliography may be found in Bimson, *Redating,* pp. 67 – 74.

Although the late-date theory is highly popular today, the arguments upon which it rests are not as strong as they appear at first glance. While it is beyond the scope of the present work to examine them in detail,[20] we must briefly consider the strengths and weaknesses of each of these arguments.

1. From the very outset, the search for evidence of the Hebrew conquest of Canaan has been based on a false assumption. It has been assumed that all the cities captured by the Israelites were burned, resulting in clear archaeological evidence in the form of layers of ash and other burnt debris. But burning was not part of the taking of every city; in fact the Bible states categorically that burning was not part of the conquest of most cities taken by the Hebrews.

The biblical record is clear in this regard: only three Palestinian cities were burned—Jericho (Josh. 6:24), Ai (Josh. 8:28), and Hazor (Josh. 11:11–13). Other captured cities were not destroyed by fire. Joshua 11:13 is worth quoting in full: "But as for the cities that stood still in their strength [Jericho and Ai had previously been burned], Israel burned none of them, save Hazor only; that did Joshua burn." Thus in seeking to establish a correlation between archaeological evidence of the burning of Canaanite cities and the conquest of Joshua, we must restrict ourselves to (a) Jericho, (b) Ai, and (c) Hazor. Evidence of burning at other sites is irrelevant.

a. Erosion of the soil and John Garstang's misinterpretations of the archaeological evidence have rendered Jericho one of the most difficult of all biblical cities to investigate.[21] Garstang's startling announcement that he had found the ruins of the city attacked by Joshua was an incorrect interpretation of his findings.[22] Kathleen Kenyon showed conclusively that the walls he identified as Late Bronze (ca. 1400 B.C., which would be consistent with the early date for the

20. Bimson's work presents the most recent refutation of the arguments for the late date.

21. See the excellent summary of the archaeology of Jericho in Bimson, *Redating,* chapter 4.

22. Ibid., pp. 118–19.

exodus) were in fact Early Bronze Age fortifications, half a millennium older than Garstang had thought.[23] It must be emphasized, however, that rejection of Garstang's conclusions does not necessarily mean rejection of 1400 as the date of the fall of Jericho; rather it means that evidence independent of Garstang's wrongly identified walls must be sought.

If Garstang's walls are not proof of an early conquest, what evidence is there of Joshua's attack? The answer is, "very little." It is virtually certain that the city fell to the Hebrews at some time during the Late Bronze Age, but erosion has removed almost all traces of Late Bronze Age Jericho. The few traces that do remain allow us to conclude with certainty that there was indeed a town at Jericho in Late Bronze times,[24] but because of the erosion we cannot say how extensive the Late Bronze settlement was. The major question to ask at this point is, when was the Late Bronze city destroyed? Kenyon's answer does not harmonize with either the early or the late date for the exodus. She dated the fall of Late Bronze Jericho to the decades around 1325 B.C.,[25] too late for a conquest in about 1400 and too early for a late exodus during the reign of Ramses II.

An interesting alternative view has been offered by Bruce K. Waltke, who wishes to push back the date of Late Bronze Jericho's fall to about 1400 B.C., in accord with an early date for the exodus.[26] Waltke contends that pottery found in the scant remains of the Late Bronze city is from the Late Bronze IIA period, 1410 – 1340 B.C. To pinpoint the date of destruction more precisely within these years, Waltke argues that no Egyptian scarabs later than the reign of Amenhotep III have been found, thus indicating a destruction before the reign of Akhenaton. Further confirmation that Jericho was destroyed

23. Kathleen Kenyon, *Archaeology in the Holy Land,* 3rd ed. (New York: Praeger Books, 1970), p. 210.

24. Ibid., pp. 210 – 11. The evidence consists of scanty remains of houses, a small quantity of pottery, and some tombs.

25. Ibid., p. 211.

26. Bruce K. Waltke, "Palestinian Artifactual Evidence Supporting the Early Date of the Exodus," *Bibliotheca Sacra* 129 (1972): 39ff.

before Akhenaton may be seen in the fact that Jericho is not mentioned in the Amarna Letters. If Waltke is correct, Late Bronze Jericho was burned by Joshua before the end of the first quarter of the fourteenth century at the latest. It must be kept in mind, however, that so little remains of the city of Joshua's day that any conclusion is extremely dangerous. All that can be said with certainty from an archaeological standpoint is that a date around 1400 for Jericho's fall is as possible as any other date which has been suggested.

b. At the present time it is impossible to conclude anything about the exodus and conquest from Ai, since the city has not been certainly identified.[27]

c. Hazor, a northern site thoroughly excavated by Yigael Yadin, was the third city burned by the incoming Hebrews. Yadin and other scholars have used the archaeological material from this city as proof of a late conquest (ca. 1230 B.C.), and hence a late exodus. It seems, however, that the use of Hazor as evidence of a late conquest is based on an arbitrary and preconceived acceptance of the late date.

It appears that this massive site suffered no fewer than three destructions by fire in the Late Bronze Age. The first burning occurred near the end of the fifteenth century, in the Late Bronze I Period. In the Upper City (Hazor is a two-level city) the town of Stratum XV represents this period, and was clearly destroyed by violence; Area H, which contained a temple, was found buried under nearly two meters of destroyed brick, and the temple was never again rebuilt. In the Lower City, the corresponding level is Stratum 2, which also suffered burning.[28] The town of Stratum 1B in the Lower City was destroyed in about 1300 B.C. The third and last destruction by fire, seen in Stratum XIII of the Upper City and 1A of the Lower, was dated by the excavators to about 1230 B.C.

Yadin correctly assigns the destruction of 1300 B.C. to a campaign of Pharaoh Seti I, but believes on the basis of his preconceived acceptance of the late date for the exodus that

27. Ibid., pp. 38 – 39.
28. Ibid., p. 43. The destruction date is indicated by ceramic evidence and by a scarab of Thutmosis IV (1415 – 1401 B.C.) found in the next level, 1B.

Joshua's attack can be seen in the destruction of 1230. Waltke has clearly demonstrated that this view is not compatible with the scriptural narrative, which states that the Hebrews took the city twice, once in the initial conquest by Joshua and again in the days of Barak and Deborah (Judg. 4).[29] The only interpretation that fits all the evidence is to attribute the 1230 burning to Barak, the 1300 destruction to Seti I, and the late-fifteenth-century attack to Joshua. If Yadin's view is accepted, there is no archaeological evidence of the events of Judges 4.

Although the interpretation of the finds at Jericho and Hazor is complex in the extreme, what has been said here will make it clear that the archaeological record does not categorically support the late date for the exodus, as is often claimed. At Jericho, despite the difficulties caused by erosion, a case can be made for an early conquest. At Hazor, the case is even stronger. At that city, the early date for the exodus provides the most natural explanation of the findings of the archaeologist's spade.

2. The reference to Hebrew bondage at the city of Ramses in Exodus 1:11 creates great difficulty for the early-date position. At issue is not whether the Israelites could have worked at this city earlier than the thirteenth century B.C., since most scholars agree that Ramses existed at least as far back as Hyksos times, although the name of the town then was Avaris and not Ramses. The problem here is rather the use of the name Ramses in Genesis and Exodus long before any king of that name lived. How could a city be named after a king who did not reign until almost two centuries later?

The easiest answer to this question is simply to deny an early exodus and accept the late date.[30] But two attempts have been made to reconcile the name Ramses with the early date.

29. Ibid., pp. 44ff.
30. Cf. Kitchen, *Ancient Orient*, pp. 57 – 58.

Royal name encircled by a cartouche.

One answer to this problem among adherents of the early date is to deny that the city was named after Ramses II at all.[31] John Rea, in an early presentation of this view, states that the name Ramses may go back to Hyksos times, since the genealogy of the Nineteenth Dynasty (of which Ramses II was a member) can be traced back to the delta and hence to the Hyksos.[32] He further argues that since the Hyksos kings had a tendency to incorporate the name of the god Re into their royal names, we might expect to find them naming a city or region "Ramses" as well.

Upon serious investigation, this view is untenable. In the first place, use of the personal name Ramses earlier than Dynasty Nineteen has never been in doubt, but furnishes no evidence in regard to the city. Individuals (other than kings) who bore the name Ramses are known from the Eighteenth Dynasty, but the name was not, as Rea implies, common as far back as Hyksos times.[33] Secondly, in Egyptian sources

31. See the presentations of this view in John Rea, "The Time of the Oppression and the Exodus," *Grace Journal* 2, no. 1 (1961): 5 – 14; Gleason L. Archer, Jr., *A Survey of Old Testament Introduction* (Chicago: Moody, 1964), pp. 207ff.; and Wood, *Survey*, pp. 93 – 94.

32. Rea, "Time," p. 10.

33. See Hermann Ranke, *Die Aegyptische Personennamen* (Gluckstädt: J. J. Augustin, 1935), vol. 1, p. 218. There is only one example earlier than Dynasty Eighteen.

Cartouche containing the name Ptolemy (from the Rosetta Stone).
Courtesy, Carl A. Stapel.

the word *Ramses* in the city name Per Ramses is written in
the royal cartouche or ring, indicating beyond question that
the town was named after a king.[34] This conclusive point
and the fact that during Hyksos times the city was known as
Avaris eliminate the possibility that the city was named Ramses for some reason other than to honor a Nineteenth-Dynasty pharaoh of that name.

It may be noted also in this connection that use of the
divine name Re in the royal names of Hyksos kings does not
indicate a special regard for that god, but only an attempt to
simulate legitimate Egyptian pharaonic nomenclature. As far
as we know, the Hyksos venerated Set as their favorite deity
rather than Re.

A more attractive explanation of the city name Ramses
from the perspective of those who hold to the early date is

34. Alan H. Gardiner, *Ancient Egyptian Onomastica* (Oxford: Oxford University,
1947), vol. 2, p. 171 .

that of Merrill F. Unger.[35] Unger theorized that the term *Ramses* replaced the older name Avaris in the scriptural text to make the account of the bondage more understandable to later readers, who would not know the location of Avaris, but would recognize the city by its new name, Ramses. Similar updating of place names can be seen in other biblical references. Unger cities an example of this in Genesis 14:14. Here Abraham pursues his enemies to a city called Dan, but we know from Joshua 19:47 and Judges 18:29 that this city's original name was Laish (Leshem) and that it was renamed Dan only after the conquest.[36] In Abraham's and Moses' time the city was called Laish, but after the name had been changed to Dan the older name was forgotten by the Israelites; Genesis 14:14 was updated to reflect this change. Unger feels that Ramses is a parallel case. If such a change took place, mention of the city of Ramses in Exodus 1:11 ceases to be a convincing argument for the late date for the exodus.

3. The view that Moses could not have confronted the pharaoh in a delta capital near Goshen at any time before Dynasty Nineteen can simply no longer be held. All of the kings who reigned in the fifteenth century (the early date for the exodus)—Thutmosis III, Amenhotep II, and Thutmosis IV—have left evidence of interest and building enterprises in Lower Egypt. We will return to this evidence in the next chapter. All we need say here is that these kings did not neglect the north and were accessible to Moses, making a fifteenth-century confrontation in the delta possible.

4. Nelson Glueck's surface explorations in the lands of the Edomites and Amorites have been said to rule out the existence of kingdoms there in the late fifteenth and fourteenth centuries. If this is true, an early exodus would be unlikely, since the Edomites and Amorites denied the Hebrews passage through their kingdoms. If those kingdoms did not exist

35. Merrill F. Unger, *Archaeology and the Old Testament* (Grand Rapids: Zondervan, 1954), pp. 149 – 50.
36. The view that two separate cities of Dan are meant is without foundation.

this early, the events described in Numbers must have occurred at a later time.

Today, however, Glueck's findings are being questioned.[37] Recent archaeological discoveries in Transjordan indicate that there may indeed have been sedentary habitation in this area in the period around 1400 B.C. Further research may negate Glueck's theory that the Edomites and Amorites were not sedentary kingdoms in Transjordan at the time. But even without such a reinterpretation, the theory that there was no settled habitation in Transjordan during the Late Bronze Age does not rule out an early exodus. It seems perfectly possible that strong nomadic kingdoms, leaving little or no archaeological trace, could indeed bar the Israelites from their territory.

It is hoped that the preceding short discussion has shown the basic weaknesses of all four of the main arguments used to defend the late date for the exodus. At the very least, they are not as ironclad as adherents of the late date would have us believe.

On the other hand, there is no good reason to reject an early date for this great event in Israel's history, a date around 1446 B.C., and a conquest beginning forty years later, about 1400 B.C. This view is based upon literal acceptance of I Kings 6:1, and in the opinion of the present writer fits the other literary and archaeological material best. The next chapter examines the events and personages of the exodus from this perspective.

---

37. See Bimson, *Redating*, pp. 67ff., for further details and references.

6

The Exodus

The People and the Events

Accepting the early date for the exodus (ca. 1446 B.C.) as best satisfying the scriptural and the extrabiblical evidence, we find that this great event occurred in the early years of Pharaoh Amenhotep II (1453 – 1415 B.C.). In chapter 4 we saw that this king fancied himself a talented athlete and warrior like his father, the great Thutmosis III. Amenhotep's boasts about his own skills and accomplishments are reminiscent of the character of the pharaoh confronted by Moses.

The Bible implies that Moses had easy access to the pharaoh when confronting him with the repeated demands to let God's people go. Since the bulk of the Hebrews resided in northern Egypt, in the land of Goshen, it would naturally follow that the meetings between Moses and the pharaoh took place in the delta. Our first task in this chapter is to investigate whether Thutmosis III, who must have been the pharaoh at the height of the oppression, and Amenhotep II, the pharaoh of the exodus, built or resided in the delta.

Thutmosis III and Amenhotep II in the Delta

It does not make sense to assume that the kings of Dynasty Eighteen neglected the Nile delta region. In their capacity as kings of Upper and Lower Egypt, the pharaohs would have been expected to show an interest in both the north and the

97

south. Further, campaigns into Palestine must of geographic necessity have been launched from northern Egypt; it is highly likely that the kings resided nearby while preparations for such operations were under way. The delta also had other advantages as an area of temporary royal residence. It was (and still is) the most agriculturally productive part of the country; and Egypt's oldest major city, Memphis, was located just south of the delta. Another advantage not to be overlooked is climate. The delta offers a welcome relief in summer from the extreme heat of Upper Egypt.

Unfortunately, on account of the high water-table relatively few archaeological monuments remain in the delta. But there is some proof that the kings of Dynasty Eighteen, and especially Thutmosis III and Amenhotep II, did not neglect the delta, but in fact built and periodically resided there, just as we would expect in view of the natural advantages of the area.

Thutmosis III was a great builder. While most of his known construction works were in Upper Egypt, he did not forsake the north. A pair of obelisks known popularly as "Cleopatra's Needles" were erected by Thutmosis at Heliopolis. One now stands in New York, and the other in London.[1] Fragments of a similar red granite obelisk have been found at Heliopolis, and now reside in the Cairo Museum.[2] A black granite statue of Thutmosis III was found at Alexandria;[3] its exact origin is not known, but it probably was not brought all the way to the Ptolemaic capital from Upper Egypt. The door jambs of the south gate of the great solar temple at Heliopolis bear the name of Thutmosis III.[4] From the same city comes a stele, dated to the forty-seventh year of Thutmosis III, which commemorates his building activities at the great solar temple.[5]

1. Bertha Porter and Rosalind L. B. Moss, *Topographical Bibliography of Ancient Egyptian Hieroglyphic Texts, Reliefs, and Paintings* (Oxford: Oxford University, 1934), vol. 4, p. 4.

2. Ibid., p. 60.

3. Ibid., p. 5.

4. Ibid., p. 61.

5. Ibid., p. 63.

Finally, a black granite door jamb of Thutmosis III was found near the Cairo citadel; it probably also came from Heliopolis.[6]

There are also scattered literary references connecting Thutmosis III with building activity in northern Egypt. One of the best examples is a papyrus referring to a dockyard of Thutmosis III at a place called Perunefer.[7] While the exact site of Perunefer is still debated, it is certain that it was located in the north.

Admittedly this list is not extensive, but neither is it exhaustive. It is presented merely to show that Thutmosis III did not abandon the delta. But it is Amenhotep II, and not Thutmosis III, who by implication was living in the delta and met Moses at the time of the exodus. And in Amenhotep's reign there was a decided increase in the number of monuments built in the north.

It is interesting to note that Amenhotep II was born in the north, at the great city of Memphis, just south of the delta. This is stated on a scarab in the collection of W. M. F. Petrie.[8] If a royal prince was born in the north, Thutmosis III must have had a royal residence there. Further information regarding Amenhotep's early life is learned from the Sphinx Stele, an inscription found at Giza which describes his athletic prowess as a youth.[9] This text places the king's early athletic accomplishments at Memphis; evidently the young ruler continued to reside in the northern city of his birth even after his accession. From other sources we learn that Amenhotep, before he became king, resided with his nurse in Perunefer.[10]

One of the most well-known of Amenhotep's officials was Ken-Amon, the son of the king's boyhood nurse. The main

6. Ibid., p. 69.

7. Labib Habachi, *Tell Basta*, Supplement to *Annales du service des antiquités de l'Egypte* (Cairo, 1957), p. 115.

8. W. M. F. Petrie, *Scarabs and Cylinders with Names* (Cairo: British School of Archaeology in Egypt, 1917), pl. XXX.

9. *Ancient Near Eastern Texts Relating to the Old Testament*, ed. James B. Pritchard (Princeton, NJ: Princeton University, 1950), pp. 243ff.

10. Wolfgang Helck, *Zur Verwaltung des Mittleren und Neuen Reichs* (Leiden: E. J. Brill, 1958), p. 366.

title held by Ken-Amon was chief steward of the king in Perunefer,[11] showing that Amenhotep had estates at that northern site which were large and important enough to require
a chief steward. Other Eighteenth-Dynasty pharaohs also had
chief stewards in the north as well as in the south.[12] These
delta estates were probably used as a summer residence, as
well as a source of income, especially in the case of Amenhotep II, who had ties with the northern part of the country
from the days of his youth.

Like his father, Amenhotep II built in the delta. He has left
several traces of construction work at Bubastis in the eastern
delta. Among the ruins of a temple at Bubastis, Edouard
Naville found a red granite block bearing the name of Amenhotep II,[13] and Labib Habachi has added a second, dedicated
to the goddess Bast, and evidently a part of a wall of that
deity's temple.[14] An inscription from Tura, dated to the fourth
year of Amenhotep II and attributed to an official named
Minmose, alludes to continued building of temples in the
north during Amenhotep's reign.[15]

The evidence presented here demonstrates that, despite
the generally meager remains in the delta region from periods before Dynasty Nineteen, Amenhotep II was born and
raised in this area, built there, had estates there, and in all
probability resided there at times, at least in his early regnal
years. Thus, in accord with the early date for the exodus, it
is quite plausible to picture Moses confronting Amenhotep II in this general area.

Amenhotep II and the Exodus

As we have already seen (p. 59), Amenhotep II fought only
three wars of consequence in his long reign, probably in 1450,

11. Norman de Garis Davies, *The Tomb of Ken-Amun at Thebes* (New York:
Metropolitan Museum of Art, 1930), p. 12.

12. See Charles F. Aling, "A Prosopographical Study of the Reigns of Thutmosis
IV and Amenhotep III" (Ph.D. dissertation, University of Minnesota, 1976), pp. 190ff.

13. Edouard Naville, *Bubastis* (London: Kegan Paul, Trench, Trübner and Co.,
1891), p. 30.

14. Habachi, *Tell Basta*, pp. 89ff.

15. Alan H. Gardiner, *Egypt of the Pharaohs: An Introduction* (New York: Oxford
University, 1966), p. 199.

The Valley of the Kings.

1446, and 1444 B.C. The first two were major campaigns, but it is of interest to us that the war of year nine was a minor one, the Egyptian forces not penetrating into Palestine any further than the Galilee region.[16] We thus see that the major wars of Amenhotep II took place within the first seven years of his reign, and in fact no military activity is recorded after year nine. This early end of fighting by a king who went out of his way to boast of his talents in military areas is difficult to understand without taking into account the events recorded in the Book of Exodus. The explanation of Amenhotep's cessation of campaigning may be found in Exodus 14:5 – 28. We read that the pharaoh pursued the departing Hebrews with an army including six hundred chariots, and that this host followed the Israelites along the path opened by God through the waters of the Red Sea. When the Egyptians were in the midst of the sea, Moses at God's command stretched out his hand over the sea, and the waters returned to their normal position, destroying the chariots and soldiers of the pharaoh (v. 28). Amenhotep II never fought another major war simply because he was incapable of doing so; the loss of six

16. Ibid., pp. 202ff.

Sarcophagus of Amenhotep II, probable pharaoh of the exodus.

hundred chariots certainly crippled his army and prevented massive campaigns on the scale of those of the king's early years. But what of the pharaoh himself? Was he also drowned?

Amenhotep II ruled for more than thirty-five years (1453 – 1415), even though the exodus occurred in about 1446 B.C., his seventh regnal year. When he died, he was buried in a rock-cut tomb in the Theban necropolis like the other kings of his dynasty, and his mummy has been preserved to the present day. How can this be reconciled with the popular theory that the pharaoh of the exodus perished in the waters of the Red Sea with his soldiers?

The fact is that the Bible simply does not say that the pharaoh drowned. Exodus 14:28 tells us that the pharaoh's army was totally obliterated, but says nothing of the king himself. The view that the king was also drowned is derived not from the Exodus account at all, but from Psalm 136:13 – 15: "To him which divided the Red Sea into parts: for his mercy endureth for ever: and made Israel to pass through the midst of it: for his mercy endureth for ever: But overthrew Pharaoh and his host in the Red Sea: for his mercy endureth for ever." The point made by the psalmist is that God delivered

Israel and punished the Egyptians; no attempt is being made to present minute details of the events described. To say that the pharaoh was overthrown in the Red Sea is in no way proof that Amenhotep II drowned. It is a figure of speech. We use the same type of statement when we say, for example, that Hitler was defeated in Russia. We do not mean that the man Adolf Hitler lost his life in Russia; we mean that his armies were defeated there. Hitler himself did not die on the battlefields of the Soviet Union, but died by his own hand in his bunker in Berlin. Without confirmation in the Exodus account, we have no right to use Psalm 136:15 to claim that the pharaoh drowned.

The Ten Plagues

There are several recent and authoritative English accounts of the biblical plagues in the light of Egyptology, making a detailed discussion here unnecessary.[17] We will limit our treatment to some observations not often made by previous authors.

It is often asked whether there are any Egyptian records mentioning the plagues, and, if not, why none exist. The answer is that there are no such references, but neither should we expect any. The peoples of the ancient Near East kept historical records to impress their gods and also potential enemies, and therefore rarely, if ever, mentioned defeats or catastrophes. Records of disasters would not enhance the reputation of the Egyptians in the eyes of their gods, nor make their enemies more afraid of their military might.

Only in the case of the last plague, the death of the first-born sons, can we expect any Egyptian evidence. This plague extended to the family of the pharaoh himself. Since we know a good deal about the royal families of Dynasty Eighteen, we can investigate to see whether Amenhotep II was succeeded

---

17. See John J. Davis, *Moses and the Gods of Egypt* (Grand Rapids: Baker, 1971), pp. 84ff.; or Kenneth A. Kitchen, "Plagues of Egypt," *New Bible Dictionary,* ed. J. D. Douglas (Grand Rapids: Eerdmans, 1962), pp. 1001 – 03.

by his eldest son, or by another son, as we should expect in the light of the last plague.

A stele[18] set up between the forepaws of the great Sphinx at Giza by Amenhotep's successor, Thutmosis IV, is often cited as evidence of the death of Amenhotep's firstborn.[19] In this document Thutmosis tells of an incident in his youth before he became king. He was hunting in the vicinity of the Sphinx, and while resting by that venerable but sand-covered monument, the prince had a dream. The solar deity represented by the Sphinx promised him that if he would remove the sand around the statue, Thutmosis would some day be king. The startled youth complied with this request, and eventually succeeded his father as Thutmosis IV. The implication of this text is obvious. At some time during his youth, Thutmosis was not the eldest living son of Amenhotep II, and thus had little hope of inheriting Egypt's throne. It would seem, therefore, that we have in this account a confirmation of the tenth plague. Thutmosis had an elder brother, and did not expect to be king; but that brother died in the last plague, and Thutmosis became crown prince.

Unfortunately, closer examination of the evidence does not allow us to use the Sphinx Stele as proof of the tenth plague.[20] Thutmosis IV began to reign no earlier than 1415 B.C. and died in 1401. His mummy shows him to have been about twenty-nine at his death; therefore, he was born in about 1430, more than a decade after the events described in the Book of Exodus.

There is, however, some evidence of the final plague without resort to the Sphinx Stele of Thutmosis IV. Thutmosis is

18. James H. Breasted, *Ancient Records of Egypt* (Chicago: University of Chicago, 1906), vol. 2, par. 810 – 15.

19. See Merrill F. Unger, *Archaeology and the Old Testament* (Grand Rapids: Zondervan, 1954), pp. 142 – 43; Gleason L. Archer, Jr., *A Survey of Old Testament Introduction* (Chicago: Moody, 1964), p. 218; and, most recently, Leon Wood, *A Survey of Israel's History* (Grand Rapids: Zondervan, 1970), p. 128.

20. On all of this see Charles F. Aling, "The Sphinx Stele of Thutmose IV and the Date of the Exodus," *Journal of the Evangelical Theological Society* 22 (June, 1979): 97 – 101.

known to have had a number of older brothers.[21] A certain Khaemwaset is known to have held military office under his father Amenhotep II, and to have been married. A second son, Webensenu, also held high military rank. Like Khaemwaset, Webensenu obviously never lived to become king. In the case of the latter, it is certain that he died before Amenhotep II, for he was buried in his father's tomb (a king's tomb was sealed immediately upon burial). A third prince, Amenhotep, is known from a dated document to have been a grown man in year twenty of his father's reign (1433 B.C.). He was a priest of the Memphite deity Ptah. Again as is the case with the other two brothers, he did not survive into the reign of Thutmosis IV.

From these facts a hypothetical reconstruction of events can be made. Webensenu was probably the firstborn son of Amenhotep II, since he was granted the privilege of burial in the royal tomb of his father. It is reasonable to regard this prince as the son of Amenhotep II killed in the tenth plague, for he never lived, as far as we know, to marriageable age. Amenhotep was probably next in age, and reached a mature enough age to hold a responsible priesthood at Memphis. He was certainly older than Thutmosis, for Thutmosis was born in about 1430 B.C. We also know that prince Amenhotep died before Amenhotep II, for Thutmosis eventually received the title of the king's eldest son, a title he could not have held if any of his older brothers were living. It is reasonable to see in prince Amenhotep the elder brother who the young Thutmosis, at the time of his dream beside the Sphinx, thought would be the next king but who died sometime before Amenhotep II, thus making Thutmosis IV the heir to the throne. Of Khaemwaset little can be said. Where he fits we do not know; whether he was older or younger than Thutmosis we can only guess. All that is certain is that he did not become king; perhaps he died also, like his two brothers, before Amenhotep II.

21. Ibid., pp. 99ff., for details and references.

The question often arises whether Exodus 12:12 ought to be interpreted to mean that each of the ten biblical plagues attacked an individual god of the Egyptian pantheon. The entire phenomenon of the plagues certainly made a mockery of Egypt's religious system, for the pagan gods were powerless to protect their worshipers; but it seems doubtful that each separate plague was directed against a different deity. The plain fact of the matter is that some of the plagues (the first, second, seventh, ninth, and tenth) appear to attack individual gods while others do not (the third, fourth, sixth, and eighth).

In the first plague the Nile was turned to blood. Although this plague was basically a blow against Egypt's water supply, it was also quite obviously an attack against the Nile god, Hapi. The god and the river were synonymous; by becoming blood, the river lost its ability to bring life and fertility to the land. Hapi was rendered powerless.

The second plague inundated the land with frogs. Egypt had a number of frog (or perhaps toad) deities, the most popular of which was probably Hekat, a goddess of childbirth. The plague certainly mocked her function. Frogs, associated with the fertility goddess, became exceptionally and disgustingly abundant.

The seventh plague, hail and severe thunderstorms, was directed against the crops of Egypt. This plague was mainly intended to cripple Egypt's economy, which was based on the land's amazing agricultural productivity. It may also be seen as an attack on the gods of Egypt who were considered responsible for that productivity, primarily Re and other solar deities, and Osiris, a god of the dead who was intimately connected with grain.

In the ninth plague darkness of great magnitude came over Egypt. This was the paramount attack on Egypt's sun god Amon-Re, and on all other less important solar deities. The sun god was powerless to shine through the darkness, a phenomenon which must have been unusually terrifying to the Egyptians, since theirs was a country where even cloud cover was a rarity. This darkness cannot be understood as an eclipse. The Egyptians knew of eclipses and did not fear them; also, the thick darkness of this plague was more oppressive than any eclipse.

The tenth plague, the death of the firstborn, attacked Egypt's living god, the pharaoh. The god-king was unable, despite his supposed divinity, to prevent the death of his own son, who died like all the other firstborn of the land. The god-king was shown here to be no stronger than his lowest subject.

The fifth plague is a special case. This plague brought disease and death to a large number of Egypt's livestock, including cattle, horses, asses, camels, oxen, and sheep. The list of affected animals in Exodus 9:3 is interesting, for the order in which the beasts appear is not random. The animals are listed in order of their importance, from cattle (the most important) to sheep (the least important). Cattle were highly valued by the ancient Egyptians, being associated with agricultural wealth. The title *overseer of cattle* was conferred on some of the highest officials of the land. The kings and the great temples measured their wealth at least partially in numbers of cattle. Horses, listed second in verse 3, were of course important for their military role. The days of the exodus were the great days of chariot warfare, and horses were as vital for the armies of Eighteenth-Dynasty Egypt as oil is to our modern military machines. The next animals mentioned, asses, were the chief beasts of burden throughout the second millennium. Only after 1000 B.C. did the ass give place to the camel. Camels, oxen, and sheep are at the end of the list, since they were far less important than the other animals named. Sheep correctly occupy the final position; they were unpopular in ancient Egypt.

While it is true that several Egyptian deities were associated with the cow (primarily the goddess Hathor), it is perhaps best not to view this plague as an attack on specific deities. We would be hard pressed to discover a horse or ass deity in any way prominent in Egyptian worship. Whether such gods existed at all is a matter of conjecture, and there was certainly no camel deity. The common denominator among these animals is surely economic and not religious.

The plague was a blow aimed at Egypt's livestock, and any attack on Egyptian religion was purely secondary. This plague should probably not be regarded as an attack on Egyptian gods.

The other four plagues are definitely not to be regarded as attacks on particular gods or goddesses of ancient Egypt. In the third plague the dust of Egypt was turned into some type of insect, probably either gnats or mosquitoes.[22] The purpose of this plague seems to have been twofold. First, it obviously brought discomfort to the population of Egypt. Second, as John Davis points out, this plague made a mockery of the personal cleanliness which was so important to the priests of Egypt.[23] But the third plague attacked no specific god or goddess. The only insect the Egyptians connected with their gods was the dung beetle, which was associated with the solar cult; and the beetle played no part at all in the third plague.

The fourth plague was a covering of the land of Egypt with what the Hebrew text calls "swarms"; this can refer only to flies in unprecedented numbers. Flies would of course bring discomfort as they infested the land, and a further dimension is added by the fact that flies carry disease. It is virtually certain that the "boils with blains" of the sixth plague refers to skin anthrax carried by the flies of the fourth plague.[24] No fly god existed in Egypt; therefore, no specific deity was attacked by the fourth plague. Nor was the sixth plague an attack on any individual god or goddess of Egypt. Its effects were obviously directed against Egypt's human population, not its deities.

Finally, the eighth plague, the plague of locusts, must be assigned to the category of plagues which did not mock any specific Egyptian deity. The Egyptians disliked locusts and did not worship them; the most common Egyptian word for grasshopper is in fact best translated by the English phrase

22. Davis, *Moses*, p. 103.
23. Ibid., pp. 103 – 04.
24. Kitchen, "Plagues," p. 1002.

"son of robbery,"[25] and shows the disgust with which the Egyptians viewed this insect. This plague was mainly economic, not directed at any god.

Final Observations on the Exodus and Conquest

We will make no attempt here to discuss the difficult question of the route of the exodus. The subject has never been satisfactorily resolved, and details remain a matter of conjecture. Many of the places mentioned in the Bible still await identification.

One important footnote to the conquest of the Promised Land must be added. The Amarna Letters, diplomatic correspondence coming in the main from the reign of Akhenaton (1364 – 1347 B.C.), tell of attacks on some of Syria-Palestine's cities by raiders known as the Habiru. Superficially, the words *Habiru* and *Hebrew* appear to be similar, and this has led some scholars to identify these raiders with the advancing Israelites under Joshua.[26]

For a number of reasons such an equation cannot be accepted, however tempting it may be to find in it extrabiblical literary evidence of the conquest.[27] First, there are severe linguistic difficulties in equating the terms *Habiru* and *Hebrew*; they are not by any means identical. Second, the Habiru as conquerors exhibited major differences from the Israelites. The Habiru operated in small marauding bands and not in massive armies like the biblical Hebrews. When they took a city, they tended, unlike the Israelites, to move on without making any attempt to settle it. Nor was the main Habiru activity in the areas where Joshua made his major efforts. Third, none of the well-known Hebrew names appear in the

25. Adolf Erman and Hermann Grapow, *Wörterbuch der Aegyptischen Sprache* (Berlin: Akademie Verlag, 1926 – 1931), vol. 3, p. 461.

26. So J. W. Jack, *The Date of the Exodus* (Edinburgh: T. and T. Clark, 1925), pp. 237 – 41.

27. For the details of what follows as well as for additional reasons, see Meredith Kline, "The HA-BI-RU—Kin or Foe of Israel?" *Westminster Theological Journal* 20 (November, 1957): 46ff.

Amarna Letters as leaders among the Habiru. Their leaders are totally different individuals. Fourth, the Habiru did not appear on the Palestinian scene suddenly in the reign of Akhenaton. They are known to have been in the area earlier, in the days when the Israelites were still in bondage in Egypt. Finally, equation of the Hebrews with the Habiru poses another serious chronological problem. The tendency among many Egyptologists in recent years has been to lower the dates for Akhenaton's reign and hence for the bulk of the Amarna Letters as well. At one time it appeared that Akhenaton was reigning already in 1400 B.C., but it now seems more probable that his father Amenhotep III was only just commencing his own reign at that time. Thus, Joshua's work in Palestine had been completed for several decades by the time of the writing of the Amarna Letters. It is best to see no connection between the Habiru and the biblical Hebrews.

7

Israel and Later Egyptian History

The Late New Kingdom: Dynasties Nineteen and Twenty

The Nineteenth Dynasty (1304 – 1200 B.C.)

The death of Horemhab in about 1304 B.C. brought the great Eighteenth Dynasty to a close; Horemhab appointed his vizier to succeed him, and this man, the founder of the new dynasty, ruled briefly as Ramses I (1304 – 1302). The new dynastic family seems to have originated in the delta; in any case, Egypt recovered from the problems of the religious revolution of the late Eighteenth Dynasty and entered a new and final period of greatness.

The first of the great kings of Dynasty Nineteen was Seti I (1302 – 1290), the son of Ramses I. In his rather short reign Seti did much to restore Egypt's position as a leading military power of the Near Eastern world.[1] Seti I fought four campaigns. The first penetrated deep into Palestine, along the coastal plain and into the Esdraelon Plain, ultimately reaching Beth-shan. Hamath, Acre, and Tyre also fell to the Egyptians. The second campaign included the reduction of Kadesh on the Orontes. The third was a western campaign against

---

1. For details see R. O. Faulkner, *Egypt: From the Inception of the Nineteenth Dynasty to the Death of Ramesses III* (New York: Cambridge University, 1966).

the Libyans, but the fourth was fought once again in Syria, this time against a newly emerging Anatolian power, the Hittites. This campaign was the beginning of a generation of trouble between the two great empires.

At home, Seti I was an active builder in the tradition of Egypt's great pharaohs. The beginning of construction of the famous Hypostyle Hall at Karnak and extensive building at the temple complex of Osiris at Abydos show that Egypt's

Temple of Seti I at Abydos.

Ceiling painting: tomb of Seti I.

Hypostyle Hall at Karnak.

prosperity had returned to a level comparable to that of the middle Eighteenth Dynasty.

Ramses II (1290 – 1223), son and successor of Seti I, was the greatest figure of his age, and was perhaps Egypt's most important king after Thutmosis III.[2] His most well-known battle was fought against the Hittites at Kadesh in 1285 B.C. The battle was an Egyptian attempt to check Hittite expansion into north Syria. If we may believe the claims of Ramses II, utter defeat at Kadesh was avoided only by the personal bravery of the pharaoh, who narrowly escaped a Hittite am-

2. Ibid., pp. 11ff.

Cartouche of Ramses II.

bush. In any case, the battle was of uncertain outcome, and Hittite hegemony over northern Syria was not ended; some years after Kadesh Egypt and the Hittites signed a treaty, however. Other wars of Ramses II included several raids into the Negev and Transjordan regions and a vigorous defense of the delta when the Libyans invaded.

The fame of Ramses II probably stems more from his impressive building operations than from anything else.[3] In all probability, he erected more structures than any other king of Egypt, including temples at Abu Simbel in the south, Abydos, and Memphis. He added massive sections to the temples of Amon-Re at Karnak and Luxor, and west of the Nile at Thebes built a large funerary temple known today as the Rameseum.

Ramses II reigned so long that when he died (after sixty-seven years of rule) he was succeeded by his thirteenth oldest son, Merneptah. There are two noteworthy events from the reign of Merneptah (1223 – 1214): his Palestinian war and his defense of Egypt against the first incursion of the so-called Sea Peoples.

We have already had occasion to cite the Palestinian campaign of Merneptah because of the mention of Israel as a defeated nation in the king's hymn of victory describing this war (p. 79). While it is certain that Merneptah actually campaigned in Syria-Palestine,[4] the statement that Israel was dev-

3. Ibid., pp. 16ff.

4. Ibid., p. 20; Kenneth A. Kitchen, *Ancient Orient and Old Testament* (Downers Grove, IL: Inter-Varsity, 1966), p. 60.

The Rameseum.

astated and was without seed need not be taken literally. It should be remembered that the statement comes from a poetic text and not from a historical inscription; all we need accept is that some part of Israelite territory was ravaged by an Egyptian army.

Of equal interest is the joint invasion of the delta by the Libyans and the "Peoples of the Sea" in the fifth year of Merneptah. The Sea Peoples, in this case comprising the Sherden, Sheklesh, Lukka, Tursha, and Akawasha, came from the Aegean world.[5] They were the first wave of a mass migration of

5. Faulkner, *Nineteenth Dynasty*, p. 19.

Columns of the Rameseum.

people that would shake the world of Egypt, Anatolia, and Syria-Palestine to its very foundations in the half century following Merneptah's reign. The pharaoh successfully averted their attempt to conquer Egypt.

The last days of Dynasty Nineteen are poorly known; all that is certain is that these were times of intrigue, dynastic struggle, and weakness. No individual kings of this period are worthy of comment here. About 1200 B.C., after the reign of Queen Tewosret (the fourth woman in Egyptian history to sit on the throne of the pharaohs), the dynasty vanished.

Despite the fact that several rulers of the Nineteenth Dynasty fought wars in Palestine, no mention of these campaigns is made in the Bible. This seeming biblical ignorance of the wars of Seti, Ramses II, and Merneptah has long puzzled scholars, and has elicited a number of explanations.[6]

The most convincing answer to this question is that of Leon Wood, who states that the Egyptian campaigns simply did not concern the Hebrew authors.[7] The Book of Judges, where we would expect to find mention of the Egyptian wars, was not written to be a detailed historical record, but was intended to be an account of the spiritual high and low points of the tribes of Israel, and of God's punishment of Israel's sin through the use of oppressive pagan nations. Egypt played no role in the divine punishment, and so was left out of the account. Further, Wood points out that the areas through and in which the Egyptians campaigned (the coast and the Esdraelon Plain) were not major sites of Israelite occupation.

The Twentieth Dynasty (ca. 1200 – 1085 B.C.)

The main king of Dynasty Twenty was its second ruler, the great Ramses III (1198 – 1167). In foreign affairs his main achievement was the defense of Egypt against the major assaults of the Libyans and the Sea Peoples, who invaded the delta three times between the king's fifth and eleventh regnal years.[8] Upon winning these wars depended Egypt's very survival, and Ramses III must be given the credit for saving his nation. The Hittite Empire was not so lucky; it succumbed to the Sea Peoples in about 1190 B.C. Many Syro-Palestinian cities (including Ugarit) also suffered destruction during these invasions.

Ramses III recorded his victories on the walls of his magnificent funerary temple at Medinet Habu, west of the Nile

6. For a good summary of the various views see John J. Bimson, *Redating the Exodus and Conquest*, Journal for the Study of the Old Testament 5 (Sheffield, 1978), pp. 76ff.

7. Leon Wood, *The Distressing Days of the Judges* (Grand Rapids: Zondervan, 1975), pp. 87 – 88.

8. Faulkner, *Nineteenth Dynasty*, pp. 27ff.

Medinet Habu—mortuary temple of Ramses III.

at Thebes. Many of the specific Sea Peoples named are already familiar to us from Merneptah's inscriptions; but one of the new groups is of extreme interest to students of the Bible—the Plst, who are certainly the Philistines of the Old Testament. They appeared en masse in the Levant in about 1190, as a part of the Sea Peoples, and first played a major role in Israelite history in the days of the judges, a period corresponding chronologically to the Egyptian Twentieth Dynasty.

There is nothing biblically noteworthy about the remaining kings of the Twentieth Dynasty (Ramses IV – XI). Egypt, exhausted by its struggle with the Sea Peoples, declined from the status of a world power. Each ruler of the dynasty took the name Ramses, reflecting the stagnant quality of Egyptian politics. Instead of looking to the future, the kings, as is shown by their imitation of Ramses II and III in their choice of names, looked only to Egypt's glorious past. None of the later kings bore the illustrious name with exceptional credit. Finally, the Twentieth Dynasty died out, and with its end came a breakdown of Egyptian unity. The kings of the Twenty-first

Relief showing captive Philistines (Medinet Habu). *Courtesy, Keith N. Schoville.*

Dynasty controlled the delta only, while the high priests of Amon exercised near royal authority in Upper Egypt. The pharaohs of this period ruled from Tanis in the delta; neither they personally nor the Egypt of their day can make any claim to real greatness.[9]

The Philistines

The Philistines, one of the Sea Peoples and a constant enemy of Israel through the period of the judges and on into the united monarchy, arrived in Palestine at the same time that the Sea Peoples invaded Egypt (ca. 1190 B.C.). They seem to have settled along the coast after their repulse at the hands of Ramses III; perhaps the Egyptians allowed and encouraged their settlement in Palestine. Of the five cities which became major Philistine centers, only Ashdod has been excavated.[10] Findings there and at other cities having sizable Philistine populations provide clues to the complex problem of Philistine origins: their pottery and architecture exhibit definite ties with the Aegean world.[11]

9. For a survey of this period see Kenneth A. Kitchen, *The Third Intermediate Period in Egypt* (Warminster: Aris and Phillips, 1972), pp. 255ff.

10. For a summary of findings, see Moshe Dothan, "Ashdod of the Philistines," in *New Directions in Biblical Archaeology*, ed. David Noel Freedman and Jonas C. Greenfield (Garden City, NY: Doubleday, 1971), pp. 17 – 27.

11. Kenneth A. Kitchen, "The Philistines," in *Peoples of Old Testament Times*, ed. D. J. Wiseman (New York: Oxford University, 1973), p. 61.

The Bible states that the Philistines came to the Levant from Caphtor (Jer. 47:4; Amos 9:7; cf. Deut. 2:23). It is now quite certain that Caphtor (Egyptian, Keftiu) was the island of Crete,[12] but we need not conclude that Crete was the original homeland of the Philistines. Amos 9:7 parallels the coming of the Philistines from Caphtor with the exodus of Israel from Egypt, and Egypt was certainly not the original homeland of the Hebrew tribes. Caphtor may have been a temporary stopping place for the Philistines midway between their place of origin farther north and the biblical world of Egypt and Palestine.

There is in fact good evidence for seeking the place of origin of the Philistines in Asia Minor. The type of feathered headdress associated with the Philistines (and with other Sea Peoples)[13] was worn in Caria, in southwest Anatolia. Further, certain Philistine words and proper names have Anatolian connections.[14] Perhaps the clearest example is the name of the best-known Philistine of all, Goliath, which is similar to the Lydian name Alyattes. Finally, there is scriptural evidence (I Sam. 7:11) that the Philistines worshiped a deity called Car, as did the inhabitants of Caria in southwest Asia Minor. Seemingly the incoming Philistines brought with them a deity from their homeland.

One thing is quite clear: the Philistines had connections with the Aegean world, connections which extended far beyond Crete. Little or nothing has been found on that island which can be in any way interpreted as Philistine; the much-discussed Phaistos Disk was almost certainly an import to Crete. The relevant biblical passages must mean the Philistines came to the Levant by way of Crete; how long they spent on the island is not known.

Solomon and Egypt

Israel moved steadily in the direction of centralized government during the last quarter of the second millennium

12. Ibid., pp. 54 – 56.
13. Ibid., p. 57.
14. Ibid., p. 67.

B.C., finally achieving full unification under David (1010 – 970) and Solomon (970 – 930). The period of the united monarchy was a glorious one, as is reflected by the military successes of David and the peacetime accomplishments of Solomon.

Under Solomon, Israel temporarily found itself one of the major powers of the Near Eastern world. This was due not only to Solomon's wealth and wisdom; it was also a result of the weakness of the larger nations. Assyria was not yet ready to expand into Syria-Palestine; the power of the Philistines had waned, thanks to David's vigorous warfare; and Egypt was weaker than it had been for many years. Solomon was as strong a monarch as any in his world. This is illustrated by his relations with Egypt.

I Kings 3:1 states that Solomon and one of Egypt's kings made an alliance, which was cemented by a diplomatic marriage between Israel's king and a daughter of the reigning pharaoh. This shows the unprecedented power and importance of Israel at the time. Normally, it was the practice of Egypt's kings to receive the daughters of other rulers into their own harems, not to give their own daughters in marriage to foreign kings. The granting of an Egyptian princess to Solomon was a major concession by the pharaoh; it shows that he treated Israel as an equal.

Kenneth Kitchen has shown that the king of Egypt who became Solomon's father-in-law could have been none other than Siamun, the sixth king of Dynasty Twenty-one, who reigned from 978 to 959.[15] The Bible states that the king of Egypt captured and gave to Solomon the Philistine town of Gezer (I Kings 9:16). This indicates that Siamun was the king concerned, for a relief from the temple of Amon at Tanis depicts Siamun smiting prisoners of war whose primary weapon was the Aegean-Anatolian double ax. Although these enemies are not named, there can be little doubt that the relief represents a campaign of Siamun into Philistine territory.[16] Siamun evidently found it to his political advantage to be Solomon's friend and ally; hence the marriage alliance.

15. Kitchen, *Third Intermediate Period*, pp. 280 – 83.
16. Ibid., p. 281.

8

Cultural Contacts Between Egypt and Israel

It is to be expected that when two nations share a common border, as did ancient Israel and Egypt, each nation will exert some cultural influence upon the other. Normally, the stronger and more advanced state takes the lead in exerting such influence; but the smaller country can also make its influence felt. Mutual cultural borrowing between Egypt and the Hebrews was further stimulated by Israel's four-hundred-year residence in Egypt, and by the flight of some Jews to the Nile Valley at the time of the Babylonian captivity.

Israel's Debt to Egypt

Many elements of the advanced civilization of the Nile Valley were borrowed by the Hebrews; it is impossible to mention more than a few of them here (on most of the following points we are heavily indebted to the work of the Canadian scholar Ronald J. Williams). Let it be said at the outset that the present author regards Israel's unique religious beliefs to be the product of divine inspiration and not cultural borrowing.

Linguistic Borrowing

Williams has assembled a number of examples of common Egyptian idiomatic phrases which have been carried over into Hebrew and which appear in the Old Testament:[1]

1. In Ecclesiastes 4:8, reference is made to a person who does not have a "second," meaning a companion or fellow. The use of the term *second* to mean "companion" is purely Egyptian; it does not occur elsewhere in known Hebrew literature.[2]

2. In I Kings 18:42, the prophet Elijah is said to have put his face between his knees as a gesture of sadness and mourning. The same idiom has been found in Ugaritic literature, but ultimately the phrase is Egyptian; it is the most common Egyptian expression for being in a state of mourning.[3]

3. Lamentations 4:20, referring to King Zedekiah, calls the Hebrew king the "breath of our nostrils." This description of a king, though unique in Hebrew literature, is shown by Williams to have been well known in Egyptian texts describing the pharaoh. Ramses II, for example, is specifically called the "breath of our nostrils" in an inscription from Abydos.[4]

4. Proverbs 17:27 provides an example of a Hebrew phrase which is difficul* to interpret without knowledge of its Egyptian origin. The Hebrew text speaks of a man of understanding having a "cool spirit"; the phrase is unique, not occurring anywhere else in Hebrew literature. Williams observes that the Egyptians used the terms *hot* and *cold* to mean "passionate" and "calm," respectively. Thus, the statement in Proverbs means that a man of understanding has a calm spirit.[5]

Beyond the Egyptian idioms appearing in the Old Testa-

1. Cf. Ronald J. Williams, "Egypt and Israel," in J. R. Harris, ed., *The Legacy of Egypt* (New York: Oxford University, 1971), pp. 264 – 65; and idem, "Some Egyptianisms in the Old Testament," in Gerald E. Kadish, ed., *Studies in Honor of John A. Wilson,* Studies in Ancient Oriental Civilization 35 (Chicago: University of Chicago, 1969), pp. 93 – 98.
2. Williams, "Egypt and Israel," p. 264.
3. Ibid., p. 265.
4. Williams, "Some Egyptianisms," p. 93.
5. Ibid., p. 97.

ment, Williams also has found a number of metaphors borrowed by the Hebrew authors of the Bible. The most striking example of an Egyptian metaphor in the Bible is the description of God as a potter who shapes the lives of men (Job 10:9; 33:6; Isa. 29:16; 45:9; 64:8; Jer. 18:2—6). This phrase had its origin in the religious and wisdom literature of Egypt (where it was of course used of pagan gods), was borrowed by the Old Testament writers, and eventually found its way into the New Testament (Rom. 9:21).[6]

Many transliterated Egyptian words also made their way into Hebrew. This is to be expected, given the close interaction between the two nations. *Pharaoh* is certainly the most common of these words; *ḥarṭōm*, meaning "magician," is another. *Shūshan*, meaning basically "lily" or "blossom," is from Egyptian *sšn*, "lotus." *Shēsh*, "white marble," is from Egyptian *šs*, "alabaster." Hebrew *sūph*, "reeds," is derived from Egyptian *ṯwfy*, with identical meaning. These few examples must suffice, but the list could be greatly extended.[7]

And finally, considering the Hebrew sojourn in Egypt, it should come as no surprise that several Egyptian proper names are found among the Hebrews of the Old Testament, especially among Israelites who lived either through part of the bondage or shortly after the exodus.[8]

1. *Moses* comes from the Egyptian verb *ms*, "to bear a child." Normally, such a root would have been combined with the name of a deity, as in Ramses, Amenmeses, and Thutmosis.
2. Hebrew *Phinehas* is derived from Egyptian *pʒ nḥsy*, "the Negro."
3. Hebrew *Hophni* originated in Egypt as *ḥfnr*, "the tadpole."
4. *Merari* is Egyptian *mrry*, "beloved."

6. Williams, "Egypt and Israel," p. 268.

7. Ibid., pp. 263 — 64; see also Adolf Erman and Hermann Grapow, *Wörterbuch der Aegyptischen Sprache* (Berlin: Akademie Verlag, 1926 — 1931), vol. 6, pp. 243 — 44.

8. For nos. 1 — 4, and for others, see Williams, "Egypt and Israel," pp. 262 — 63.

5. Miriam is probably derived from *mry imn,* "beloved of Amon."

Wisdom Literature

The Egyptians made an outstanding contribution in the area of wisdom literature. They placed great emphasis on the wise man, and loved to compile collections of the sayings or teachings (actual or alleged) of sages of the past.[9] Many of the best-known works are instructions in right behavior, and bear strong similarity to portions of biblical wisdom literature, particularly the Book of Proverbs.

Similarities between Proverbs and Egyptian wisdom literature extend beyond likeness of literary type; several sections of the Book of Proverbs appear to have been directly or indirectly derived from Egyptian originals. Let it be said here that this borrowing from Egyptian sources in no way detracts from the inspiration of Proverbs; truth is truth, no matter what its origin. The Egyptian maxims quoted in Proverbs are no less divinely inspired than Paul's quotations from the pagans Aratus (Acts 17:28) and Menander (I Cor. 15:33).

Two examples may be cited to illustrate the dependence of parts of Proverbs on Egyptian wisdom literature. In Proverbs 25:21—22 (and again in Rom. 12:20) there is an injunction to be kind to one's enemies, feeding them when they are hungry and giving them drink when they are thirsty. In so doing, one "heaps coals of fire" upon their heads. A similar expression occurs in a late Egyptian tale.[10] In the story of Setna, a guilty individual carries a brazier of hot coals on his head as a gesture of penance. Realizing what the Egyptians meant by the phrase aids us in interpreting the biblical passage. When we do good to our enemies, we are not bringing punishment on them, but, on the contrary, are helping them come to an attitude of repentance.

9. For discussion see Georges Posener, "Literature," in J. R. Harris, ed., *The Legacy of Egypt* (New York: Oxford University, 1971), pp. 220 – 55.
10. Williams, "Egypt and Israel," p. 267.

Another section of Proverbs derived from an Egyptian original is Proverbs 22:17–23:14. This portion of Scripture contains close paraphrases of many of the maxims found in a late-Nineteenth-Dynasty version of the "Wisdom of Amenemope," which itself originated in the Eighteenth Dynasty.[11] An example or two from the Bible and from Amenemope will show the similarity. The reader is exhorted by Amenemope to avoid financial gain, and theft of riches; ill-gotten wealth will take wings like geese and fly away into the sky. This is paralleled by Proverbs 23:4–5 where exertion for wealth and thievery of riches are also condemned; riches will make themselves wings and fly away into the sky like an eagle. In a second example, Amenemope challenges his audience: "Give your ears and hear [the words which are] said, give your mind over to their interpretation; it is profitable to put them in your heart, but woe to him that neglects them!"[12] Substantially the same thought is presented in Proverbs 22:17.

Social and Political Institutions

We would expect to find that Egypt's highly organized bureaucracy influenced the government of Israel, since that government was shaped and refined by Solomon, a king who had solid connections with Egypt. Williams has demonstrated that such was indeed the case.[13] Scribal schools of the Egyptian type were established in Jerusalem to train young men for governmental service. Beyond this, several obviously Egyptian titles are found in the Israelite bureaucracy (some of these extended back as far as the reign of David). Chief among these are the titles "royal companion" (I Chron. 27:33) and "one who is over the household" (I Kings 4:6), that is, the chief steward. Even Solomon's division of Israel's labor force

---

11. For a summary see ibid., pp. 277ff. The theory that the Egyptian text was borrowed from a Semitic original has been successfully and finally refuted by Ronald J. Williams, "The Alleged Semitic Original of the Wisdom of Amenemope," *Journal of Egyptian Archaeology* 47 (1961): 100–06.

12. William K. Simpson, ed., *The Literature of Ancient Egypt: An Anthology of Stories, Instructions, and Poetry* (New Haven, CT: Yale University, 1973), p. 244.

13. Williams, "Egypt and Israel," pp. 272–73.

into three-month shifts (I Kings 5:14) appears to have been based on Egyptian practice.

Egyptian influence is also visible in Israel's military organization. In Joshua 1:10, reference is made to the scribes of the people (the word *scribe* is often translated "officer"). The use of military scribes in the Hebrew army was most certainly modeled on Egyptian practice; the Egyptian army had an abundance of scribes at different levels.[14] One of the Egyptian military scribal officials in fact performed the very function that we see in Joshua 1:11; he published the commands of the leadership among the troops.[15]

Egypt's Debt to Israel

In few cases does cultural influence flow in one direction only. We would expect to find, perhaps to a limited extent, examples of Egyptian borrowing of some elements of the civilization of Syria-Palestine. And Williams has indeed pointed out several items adopted by Egypt from its eastern neighbors.

A number of Hebrew words and phrases were borrowed by the Egyptian language during the New Kingdom or in later periods. A Hebrew phrase meaning "footstool" appears in the New Kingdom story "Truth and Falsehood," and the Hebrew expression "fear of God" occurs uniquely in the inscriptions in the tomb of Petosiris, dated to the late fourth century B.C.[16] Some other Semitic (Hebrew and Canaanite) words found in Egyptian include *ym*, sea; *mrkbt*, chariot; *mktr*, fortress; *tpr*, scribe; *ktm*, gold; *šbd*, rod; *mkmrt*, net; *'grt*, wagon; *krr*, holocaust; *brt*, covenant; *'šg*, to misuse; and *itз*, the interrogative word "which."[17]

We have already had occasion to mention a literary motif borrowed from Israel by the Egyptians, the motif of the seven-year famine (p. 49). The Ptolemaic text recording the seven

---

14. See A. R. Schulman, *Military Rank, Title, and Organization in the Egyptian New Kingdom* (Berlin: Verlag Bruno Hessling, 1964), pp. 62ff.

15. Ibid., p. 66.

16. Williams, "Egypt and Israel," p. 265.

17. Ibid., p. 264.

years of famine places that event far too early, associating it with the reign of Djoser of Dynasty Three; but this text certainly owes its inspiration to the account of the great famine in the days of Joseph.[18]

Hebrew Monotheism and Egyptian Religion— An Invalid Connection

It was particularly fashionable at the turn of the last century and in the early years of the 1900s to find Israelite borrowings from Egypt which in reality were nothing of the kind. Zeal to discover the roots of Hebrew monotheism in the older civilizations of the Near East prompted even great scholars such as America's first professional Egyptologist James H. Breasted to find connections where none existed. Two examples, both related to Egypt's Amarna period and popularized by Breasted, may be cited.

Pharaoh Akhenaton of the Eighteenth Dynasty made active war upon many of Egypt's traditional gods, chief of whom was the Theban deity Amon-Re. The king's motives must have been political and economic in the main,[19] but the result was an organized persecution of many of Egypt's cults and their replacement with the worship of the Aton, a sun god. Breasted saw the new religion of Akhenaton as a form of monotheism, and thought that it heavily influenced the Mosaic religion of Israel.[20] But modern research has all but destroyed Breasted's theory.[21] It has been pointed out, for example, that Akhenaton's religion was not really monotheistic at all.[22] The king himself was still regarded as divine, and solar deities other than Aton continued to be venerated. Even the term *sole god*

18. Ibid., p. 271.

19. Charles F. Aling, "A Prosopographical Study of the Reigns of Thutmosis IV and Amenhotep III" (Ph.D. dissertation, University of Minnesota, 1976), chapter 10.

20. James H. Breasted, *A History of Egypt*, 2nd ed. (New York: Charles Scribner's Sons, 1946), p. 376.

21. See the assessment of Williams, "Egypt and Israel," p. 287.

22. For discussion see John A. Wilson, *The Culture of Ancient Egypt* (Chicago: University of Chicago, 1956), pp. 224ff.

as used of the Aton was not new. The same phrase had been used to describe several of Egypt's gods before the Amarna revolution, and meant basically that the god so described was without equal, not that he was the only deity. Nor did the worship of Aton have anything to do with Hebrew religion. Akhenaton's beliefs were confined, as far as we know, within a narrow court circle; among the general population of Egypt there was no broad base of belief in the Aton that could have spread to the Hebrew slaves. Also, Akhenaton's ideas seem to have lost all support within a generation; after the end of Dynasty Eighteen, little trace remained of his new religion. Further, Atonism did not have the impressive ethical content for which Hebrew religion is noted. Finally, and most importantly, according to the chronology we have adopted Moses lived before and not after Akhenaton. It is therefore as impossible to say that Moses derived his religious beliefs from the heretic king as to say that Abraham Lincoln learned his political philosophy from John F. Kennedy.

Breasted supported his view that Hebrew monotheism was of Egyptian origin by citing the similarity of a key document of Atonism, the great Sun Hymn from Tell el-Amarna, to Psalm 104.[23] There are indeed many points of resemblance; but, as John A. Wilson has observed, many of the thoughts present in the Sun Hymn can be found in Egyptian religious literature from both before and after the Amarna period, and are not the creation of Akhenaton and his scribes and priests.[24] Some of the ideas were generally present throughout the Near East, such as the idea that a god is the good shepherd of his people. It may be that the psalmist was familiar with some of the phrases used in ancient Egypt and in other Near Eastern lands to describe their deities. This is a subject which needs further research. But we can at least assert that Psalm 104 is in no way dependent upon any one specific text such as the great Sun Hymn; and if we dissociate these two texts,

23. Breasted, *History*, pp. 371ff.
24. Wilson, *Culture*, pp. 228 – 29.

we weaken the chief argument used to connect Hebrew monotheism with Egypt.

It is hoped that the brief summary given in this chapter will both stimulate and caution students of Hebrew-Egyptian cultural connections. Much cross-cultural borrowing has been discovered in the areas of language, literature, and social institutions. Egypt's far older civilization had much of value to contribute to Israel in these areas. On the other hand, the reader must be cautioned that, as we have tried to show, this borrowing was not a one-way process. Egypt took much from its neighbors. Further, it must be stressed again that Hebrew religion, while borrowing some literary types and even some specific proverbs, was the product of divine inspiration, and as such was totally and profoundly different from the religions of the surrounding nations, including Egypt.

Epilogue

It is hoped that the material presented in this small book will be both a help and an encouragement to the student of the Bible who knows little about Egyptology. Admittedly, many of the views and evidences presented are not original with the author, but have been gathered from a wide range of literature (both secular and theological) produced by the best minds in the field.

As we conclude our survey of Egypt and Old Testament history, we may look back over the ground we have covered to see again its importance for the study of Scripture. It must be stressed that the people and events of Bible times fit into a broader historical picture than is given in the pages of the Bible. A knowledge of this broader historical picture is vital to a proper understanding of the details of the biblical narrative. We cannot, to cite one example, fully appreciate God's deliverance of His people from bondage in Egypt if we do not understand that Egypt was at that time the greatest nation on the face of the earth, at the height of its power both economically and militarily. A second obvious example is the career of Joseph. Many of the details of his servitude and rise to prominence in Egypt are all too often ignored, or, worse yet, totally misinterpreted. Only through a study of Egyptian customs do otherwise obscure details come into focus.

One of the aims of this study has been to defend the biblical chronology for the sojourn and exodus. It is hoped that the reader has seen that the exodus can indeed be dated in the fifteenth century B.C., and need not be placed in the thirteenth. Joseph's career in Egypt need not be assigned to the Hyksos Period, but, like the exodus itself, fits better just where the biblical chronology places it. The serious Bible student does not need to move to either of the two extreme positions so common today: disregarding the biblical data and redating the sojourn and exodus to a later period, or accepting one of the absurd and radical (and totally unsupported by the primary evidence) revisions of Egyptian chronology. The biblical events fit best where the Old Testament places them.

Much more could have been said on all of the topics covered; it was not possible, nor, in a book intended for the general reader, was it desirable to be exhaustive. The general purpose of this book has been to renew interest in Egyptology as a tool for biblical study, and to stimulate learning and research in this field among biblical scholars. If this work will "prime the pump" in this regard, it will have been in some measure successful.

Bibliography

The following abbreviations have been used:

BASOR   *Bulletin of the American Schools of Oriental Research*
JEA   *Journal of Egyptian Archaeology*
JETS   *Journal of the Evangelical Theological Society*
JNES   *Journal of Near Eastern Studies*
JSS   *Journal of Semitic Studies*
NBD   *New Bible Dictionary*, ed. J. D. Douglas. Grand Rapids: Eerdmans, 1962
PEQ   *Palestine Exploration Quarterly*

Albright, W. F. "Archaeology and the Date of the Hebrew Conquest." *BASOR* 58 (April, 1935): 10 – 18.

_____. *From the Stone Age to Christianity.* Garden City, NY: Doubleday, 1957.

_____. "Further Light on the History of Israel from Lachish and Megiddo." *BASOR* 68 (December, 1937): 22 – 26.

_____. "The Israelite Conquest of Canaan in the Light of Archaeology." *BASOR* 74 (April, 1939): 11 – 23.

Aling, Charles F. "A Prosopographical Study of the Reigns of Thutmosis IV and Amenhotep III." Ph.D. dissertation, University of Minnesota, 1976.

_____. "The Sphinx Stele of Thutmose IV and the Date of the Exodus." *JETS* 22 (June, 1979): 97 – 101.

Archer, Gleason L., Jr. *A Survey of Old Testament Introduction.* Chicago: Moody, 1964.

Bakir, A. *Slavery in Pharaonic Egypt.* Cairo: L'Institut Français d'archéologie orientale, 1952.

Battenfield, James R. "A Consideration of the Identity of the Pharaoh of Genesis 47." *JETS* 15 (Spring, 1972): 77 – 85.

Bimson, John J. *Redating the Exodus and Conquest.* Journal for the Study of the Old Testament 5. Sheffield, 1978.

Bottero, Jean, et al. *The Near East: The Early Civilizations.* New York: Delacorte, 1967.

Breasted, James H. *Ancient Records of Egypt.* 5 vols. Chicago: University of Chicago, 1906.

————. *A History of Egypt.* 2nd ed. New York: Charles Scribner's Sons, 1946.

Bright, John. *A History of Israel.* 2nd ed. Philadelphia: Westminster, 1972.

Brinkman, John A. *A Political History of Post-Kassite Babylonia.* Analecta Orientalia 43. Rome, 1968.

Bruce, F. F. "Shamgar." *NBD*, p. 1170.

Brunner, Hellmut. *Altaegyptische Erziehung.* Wiesbaden: Otto Harrassowitz, 1957.

Davies, Norman de Garis. *A Corpus of Inscribed Egyptian Funerary Cones.* Oxford: Oxford University, 1957.

————. *The Tomb of Ken-Amun at Thebes.* Metropolitan Museum of Art Egyptian Expedition Publications 5. New York: Metropolitan Museum of Art, 1930.

————. *The Tomb of Rekh-mi-Re at Thebes.* Metropolitan Museum of Art Egyptian Expedition Publications 11. New York: Arno Press, 1973 reprint.

Davis, John J. *Moses and the Gods of Egypt.* Grand Rapids: Baker, 1971.

————. *Paradise to Prison.* Grand Rapids: Baker, 1975.

Duncan, J. G. *New Light on Hebrew Origins.* Naperville, IL: Alec R. Allenson, 1936.

Edwards, I. E. S. *The Pyramids of Egypt.* Baltimore: Penguin Books, 1947.

Emery, W. B. *Archaic Egypt.* Baltimore: Penguin Books, 1961.

Erman, Adolf. *A Handbook of Egyptian Religion.* London: Archibald Constable and Co., 1907.

————, and Hermann Grapow. *Wörterbuch der Aegyptischen Sprache.* 7 vols. Berlin: Akademie Verlag, 1926 – 1931.

Fakhry, Ahmed. *The Pyramids.* Chicago: University of Chicago, 1961.

Faulkner, R. O. *Egypt: From the Inception of the Nineteenth Dynasty to the Death of Ramesses III.* New York: Cambridge University, 1966.

Free, Joseph P. *Archaeology and Bible History.* Wheaton, IL: Scripture Press, 1962.

Freedman, David Noel, and Jonas C. Greenfield, eds. *New Directions in Biblical Archaeology.* Garden City, NY: Doubleday, 1971.

Gardiner, Alan H. *Ancient Egyptian Onomastica.* 3 vols. Oxford: Oxford University, 1947.

_____. *Egyptian Grammar: Being an Introduction to the Study of Hieroglyphics.* 3rd rev. ed. New York: Oxford University, 1957.

_____. *Egypt of the Pharaohs: An Introduction.* New York: Oxford University, 1966.

Griffiths, J. Gwyn. "The Egyptian Derivation of the Name Moses." *JNES* 12 (1953): 225 – 31.

Habachi, Labib. *Tell Basta.* Supplement to *Annales du service des antiquités de l'Egypte.* Cairo, 1957.

Harris, J. R., ed. *The Legacy of Egypt.* New York: Oxford University, 1971.

Hayes, William C. *Egypt: From the Death of Ammenemes III to Seqnenre II.* New York: Cambridge University, 1962.

_____. *Egypt: Internal Affairs from Tuthmosis I to the Death of Amenophis III.* New York: Cambridge University, 1966.

_____. *The Middle Kingdom in Egypt.* New York: Cambridge University, 1964.

_____, ed. *A Papyrus of the Late Middle Kingdom in the Brooklyn Museum.* Wilbour Monographs 5. Brooklyn: Brooklyn Museum, 1972 reprint.

Helck, Wolfgang. *Die Beziehungen Aegyptens zu Vorderasien im 3. und 2. Jahrtausend vor Christi.* Wiesbaden: Otto Harrassowitz, 1971.

_____. *Zur Verwaltung des Mittleren und Neuen Reichs.* Leiden: E. J. Brill, 1958.

Hendriksen, William. *Galatians.* Grand Rapids: Baker, 1968.

Hornung, Erik. *Untersuchungen zur Chronologie und Geschichte des Neuen Reichs.* Wiesbaden: Otto Harrassowitz, 1964.

Hurry, J. B. *Imhotep, the Vizier and Physician of King Zoser.* Oxford: Oxford University, 1926.

Jack, J. W. *The Date of the Exodus.* Edinburgh: T. and T. Clark, 1925.

Kadish, Gerald E., ed. *Studies in Honor of John A. Wilson.* Studies in Ancient Oriental Civilization 35. Chicago: University of Chicago, 1969.

Kenyon, Kathleen. *Archaeology in the Holy Land.* 3rd ed. New York: Praeger Books, 1970.

Kitchen, Kenneth A. *Ancient Orient and Old Testament.* Downers Grove, IL: Inter-Varsity, 1966.

_____. "From the Brickfields of Egypt." *Tyndale Bulletin* 27 (1976): 137 – 47.

_____. "Joseph." *NBD,* pp. 656 – 60.

_____. "Moses." *NBD,* pp. 843 – 50.

_____. "Plagues of Egypt." *NBD,* pp. 1001 – 03.

_____. "Potiphar." *NBD,* p. 1012.

_____. "Potipherah." *NBD,* p. 1012.

_____. *The Third Intermediate Period in Egypt.* Warminster: Aris and Phillips, 1972.

———. "Zaphnath-Paaneah." *NBD*, p. 1353.

Kline, Meredith. "The HA-BI-RU—Kin or Foe of Israel?" *Westminster Theological Journal* 19 (1956): 1–24; 19 (1957): 170–84; 20 (1957): 46–70.

Leupold, H. C. *Exposition of Genesis.* 2 vols. Grand Rapids: Baker, 1965.

Lichtheim, Miriam. *Ancient Egyptian Literature.* 2 vols. Berkeley: University of California, 1973, 1976.

Lucas, A., and J. R. Harris. *Ancient Egyptian Materials and Industries.* London: Edward Arnold, 1962.

Naville, Edouard. *Bubastis.* London: Kegan Paul, Trench, Trübner and Co., 1891.

Newberry, Percy E. *Beni Hasan.* 4 vols. London: Kegan Paul, Trench, Trübner and Co., 1893.

Peet, T. Eric. *Egypt and the Old Testament.* Liverpool: University of Liverpool, 1924.

Petrie, W. M. F. *Egypt and Israel.* London: Society for Promoting Christian Knowledge, 1911.

———. *Scarabs and Cylinders with Names.* Cairo: British School of Archaeology in Egypt, 1917.

Porter, Bertha, and Rosalind L. B. Moss. *Topographical Bibliography of Ancient Egyptian Hieroglyphic Texts, Reliefs, and Paintings.* 7 vols. Oxford: Oxford University, 1927–1964.

Posener, G. "Les Asiatiques en Egypte sous les XIIe et XIIIe Dynasties." *Syria* 34 (1957): 145–63.

Pritchard, James B., ed. *The Ancient Near East in Pictures.* Princeton: Princeton University, 1955.

———. *Ancient Near Eastern Texts Relating to the Old Testament.* Princeton: Princeton University, 1950.

Ranke, Hermann. *Die Aegyptische Personennamen.* 2 vols. Glückstadt: J. J. Augustin, 1935.

Rea, John. "The Time of the Oppression and the Exodus." *Grace Journal* 2, no. 1 (1961): 5–14.

Redford, D. B. "The Coregency of Tuthmosis III and Amenophis II." *JEA* 51 (1965): 107–22.

———. *History and Chronology of the Eighteenth Dynasty of Egypt.* Toronto: University of Toronto, 1967.

———. *A Study of the Biblical Story of Joseph.* Leiden: E. J. Brill, 1970.

Rowe, Alan. "The Famous Solar City of On." *PEQ* 94 (1962): 133–43.

Rowley, H. H. "Israel's Sojourn in Egypt." *Bulletin of the John Rylands Library* 22 (1936): 243–90.

Schulman, A. R. *Military Rank, Title, and Organization in the Egyptian New Kingdom.* Berlin: Verlag Bruno Hessling, 1964.

Simpson, William K., *The Literature of Ancient Egypt: An Anthology of Stories, Instructions, and Poetry.* New Haven, CT: Yale University, 1973.

Smith, Wilbur M. *Egypt in Biblical Prophecy.* Grand Rapids: Baker, 1957.

Steindorff, George, and Keith C. Seele. *When Egypt Ruled the East.* Chicago: University of Chicago, 1965.

Stigers, Harold G. *A Commentary on Genesis.* Grand Rapids: Zondervan, 1975.

Unger, Merrill F. *Archaeology and the Old Testament.* Grand Rapids: Zondervan, 1954.

Uphill, E. P. "Pithom and Ramses: Their Location and Significance." *JNES* 27 (1968): 291 – 316; 28 (1969): 15 – 39.

Van Seters, John. *The Hyksos: A New Investigation.* New Haven, CT: Yale University, 1966.

Vergote, J. *Joseph en Egypte.* Orientalia et Biblica Lovaniensia III. Louvain, 1959.

Waltke, Bruce K. "Palestinian Artifactual Evidence Supporting the Early Date of the Exodus." *Bibliotheca Sacra* 129 (1972): 33 – 47.

Ward, William A. "The Egyptian Office of Joseph." *JSS* 5 (1960): 144 – 50.

———. "Egyptian Titles in Genesis 39 – 50." *Bibliotheca Sacra* 114 (January, 1957): 40 – 59.

Wente, E. F., and C. Van Sicklen. "A Chronology of the New Kingdom." In *Studies in Honor of George R. Hughes,* ed. Janet H. Johnson, pp. 217 – 61. Studies in Ancient Oriental Civilization 39. Chicago: University of Chicago, 1976.

Williams, Ronald J. "The Alleged Semitic Original of the Wisdom of Amenemope." *JEA* 47 (1961): 100 – 06.

Wilson, John A. *The Culture of Ancient Egypt.* Chicago: University of Chicago, 1956.

Wiseman, D. J., ed. *Peoples of Old Testament Times.* New York: Oxford University, 1973.

Wood, Leon. *The Distressing Days of the Judges.* Grand Rapids: Zondervan, 1975.

———. *A Survey of Israel's History.* Grand Rapids: Zondervan, 1970.

Wright, G. Ernest. "The Epic of Conquest." *Biblical Archaeologist* 3 (1940): 25 – 40.

Subject Index

9 781532 680359